How to ...

get

Key Point

Basic concepts in point form.

Close Up

Additional hints, notes, tips or background information.

Watch Out!

Areas where problems frequently occur.

Quick Tip

Concise ideas to help you learn what you need to know.

Remember This!

Essential material for mastery of the topic.

Your Guide to ...

Accounting for Small Business

Computer & manual ledgers and books

Handling taxes, GST and employee costs

COLES NOTES have been an indispensable aid to students on five continents since 1948.

COLES NOTES now offer titles on a wide range of general interest topics as well as traditional academic subject areas and individual literary works. All COLES NOTES are written by experts in their fields and reviewed for accuracy by independent authorities and the Coles Editorial Board.

COLES NOTES provide clear, concise explanations of their subject areas. Proper use of COLES NOTES will result in a broader understanding of the topic being studied. For academic subjects, COLES NOTES are an invaluable aid for study, review and exam preparation. For literary works, COLES NOTES provide interesting interpretations and evaluations which supplement the text but are not intended as a substitute for reading the text itself. Use of the NOTES will serve not only to clarify the material being studied, but should enhance the reader's enjoyment of the topic.

© Copyright 2001 and Published by
COLES PUBLISHING. A division of Prospero Books
Toronto – Canada
Printed in Canada

Cataloguing in Publication Data
Herman, Peter 1955–

Your guide to ... accounting for small business

(Coles notes) ISBN 0-7740-0630-7

1. Small business — Accounting   I. Title.   II. Series

HF5657.H47 1999   657'.9042   C99-930126-8

Publisher: Nigel Berrisford
Editing: Paul Kropp Communications
Book design: Karen Petherick, Markham, Ontario
Layout: Richard Hunt

Manufactured by Webcom Limited
Cover finish: Webcom's Exclusive DURACOAT

Contents

Accounting for small business

Success in business requires several things – a product or service idea, a financial plan to raise the money, a marketing plan to sell and distribute the product or service and an accounting system to keep all aspects of the business honest. Without proper record keeping, the best business is doomed to fail.

Accounting means just what the word implies: to account or to hold accountable. Its purposes are twofold:

- to let you know that all of the components of your business plan are being carried out economically and profitably
- to supply you with needed information for the day-to-day operation of your business

Accounting is often referred to as the language of business. This is because some very important information about your business is often conveyed through its financial reports. Your small business's accounting system provides such information as:

- who owes your business money and how much (accounts receivable)
- whom your business owes money to (accounts payable)
- whether the business operates profitably (income statement)
- whether the business is in a strong position financially (balance sheet)
- whether the business has enough money to pay its debts and continue to operate (cash flow)

The day-to-day management of any company, large or small, requires constant reference to how much money the company has available and how much it will require. A business that does not have at least this information is running blind. This could result in financial hardship, embarrassment and the loss of credibility with customers and suppliers.

Running a small business does not require an owner to have a detailed knowledge of accounting – that can be left to accountants and bookkeepers. But the owner of a business does need to exercise financial control of the business and must be confident that any accounting records are accurate and make sense. To do this you need a basic understanding of what accounting is, how it works and the significance of the information contained in the various reports.

In addition to checking the accuracy of accounting reports, you must also be able to monitor the business's progress in achieving its financial goals. For instance, you would want to know if your company is running profitably, or whether it is losing money. You may decide that the accounts receivable are too high and that your business is carrying too much debt. Decisions of this type can only be made with the help of your accounting reports.

Accounting reports are also necessary for compliance with government requirements. As a sole proprietor, you must keep a set of financial records and receipts as well as file a T2124 statement of business income with your personal tax return. In addition, GST and PST remittances must normally be prepared quarterly or annually.

Proper attention to the accounting system and procedures will help you to:

- maximize profits
- minimize taxes
- control your cash flow
- help your business reach long-term goals

This book will provide you with a basic understanding of how information is compiled in your books and how financial reports should be read and understood, and provide an overview of the types of accounting systems available. Let's get started.

CHAPTER ONE

The basics of small business accounting

It is extremely important that a business properly account for its transactions, since accounting errors or omissions can easily translate into a loss of cash. For instance, assume that you neglect to prepare an invoice for goods you ship. The minute the goods leave the factory there is no longer any record of the transaction. You then have to rely on the good will of your customers to ensure that you get paid.

Since small business owners rarely have enough time to verify that every transaction is recorded, your accounting system should minimize the likelihood of error. This is referred to as **internal control**. A control system for sales might involve matching up customer purchase orders with sales invoices, or maintaining a shipping log and matching up information on goods shipped with invoices.

An alternative involves reviewing the reports prepared by the accounting system. This is what is normally referred to as **management override**. Since other types of controls involve the efforts of different staff members and the maintenance of additional accounting records (neither of which may be feasible for a very small business), review of accounting reports is often the best an owner can do.

STRATEGIC PLANNING AND CONTROL

One major function of an accounting system is to monitor your company's progress in achieving its long-term goals. The accounting system produces a number of different reports. Some reports –

such as **accounts receivable** and **accounts payable** listings – are more important in controlling the day-to-day management of the business. Others are more important in monitoring a company's overall progress over a period of time. These latter reports are referred to as the company's **financial statements**.

Financial statements generally include an **income statement**, a **balance sheet** and a **statement of cash flow**. They are normally prepared annually, but can also be prepared on an interim basis – monthly or quarterly. Computers make it possible to produce some reports as often as you wish. Financial statements take a snapshot of a company's financial situation, including whether or not it is earning money (income statement) and whether it is financially solid (balance sheet). In addition, such reports provide you with support for making long-term strategic decisions, such as the level of sales to be achieved, the type and level of expenses to be incurred, the type of products to offer and the type of financing the business will require. They are critical to the longevity and success of your business.

TAXES AND LEGAL REQUIREMENTS

Companies in Canada must comply with a number of different statutes. The main ones are:

- the Federal and Provincial Income Tax Acts
- various provincial sales tax acts
- various labor codes and regulations
- the corporation acts of the various provinces

Every legal statute under which business operates in Canada requires you to maintain adequate books and records. Furthermore, most acts require that records be kept on hand for a *minimum of six years*. Failure to maintain decent books is subject to penalty. Ignorance of the law is never considered an excuse. Small business owners must be responsible enough to know what records are required and ensure that they comply with those requirements. We'll discuss accounting records further in chapter 7.

Your accounting system must provide information on money owed to the government. Almost all business are required to make various government remittances on an interim basis in addition to the annual income tax filing, including:

- **Employee payroll deductions** A portion of each employee's pay is withheld and remitted to the government monthly. Late filings are heavily penalized.
- **GST/HST** The general sales tax has to be calculated and re-mitted on either a monthly, quarterly or annual basis. Your accounting system must calculate both GST paid out and GST collected by the company since only the net difference is due to the government.
- **Sales tax collection** In addition to the GST, most provinces have a provincial sales tax. These are calculated as a percent-age of total sales and are normally remitted monthly.
- **Workers Compensation** This is a payroll levy paid into an agency of the government that ensures against workplace injuries. Virtually all companies are covered by Workers Com-pensation and are obliged to make remittances on a percentage of gross payroll.

DEALING WITH BANKS AND OTHER CREDITORS

Dealing with banks is almost always a major issue in running a small business. If records are not accurate and your business appears to be disorganized, banks and other institutions may to be apprehensive about dealing with you.

Banks generally require two types of records from small busi-nesses. One is the accounts receivable listing. Normally, banks will take your customer debts as security for their advances. But to ensure that their debt is secure they want to know that it is fully covered by collectible accounts receivable. They normally need this data on a monthly basis, so accurate records have to be kept up to date.

Banks and other financial backers also insist on seeing your annual financial statements. They like to see that your company is profitable and financially stable. Things unravel quickly in business, and losses can soon add up to erode a company's financial position. If you have a line of credit or a small business loan, the bank will normally conduct an annual review of your company, which includes a review of the company's financial statements and an interview with management.

Often a company purchases much of its product from only a few suppliers – obtaining 30-, 60- or 90-day payment terms from them. Those suppliers often request a copy of the annual financial statements. In addition to analyzing the financial statements, they may also want to chat with your bank. As a result, the credibility of your organization relies on the timeliness and accuracy of the financial information prepared.

MONITORING YOUR COMPANY'S PROGRESS

The most successful small businesses work in accordance with a strategic plan. The plan usually contains a breakdown of projected sales (sales broken down by product line) and projected expenses (what costs the company needs to incur in achieving the sales). The projection process helps you manage your company by:

- forcing you to map out a strategy to achieve your objectives over the coming period,
- providing an element of control in achieving those objectives (for instance, it ensures that expenses stay within a certain limit)

Financial projections are really financial statements for a future period. They should be realistic representations of what results your company hopes to achieve with a certain strategic plan. The process includes three basic steps:

1. using best estimates in determining the likely outcome of a given course of action
2. determining what costs and revenues will relate to that course of action and preparing a set of projected financial statements
3. evaluating the outcome against the projections (at the end of the period covered by the projections, actual financial statements are compared to the projections to ensure that the business is proceeding according to plan)

The budgeting process provides yet another way in which accounting information can be used to control a small business. We'll go into this in more detail in chapter 9.

SHOULD YOU COMPUTERIZE?

In order to set up a set of books for your business, you must first decide whether or not you want to computerize. If your business does less than $100,000 in total revenue, a manual system may make more sense. A manual system will take less time to set up and is easier to use and understand for those with absolutely no computer skills.

For larger companies, or entrepreneurs comfortable with computers, there is a host of user-friendly software available for the novice. The software is set up to minimize the need for specialized expertise and can provide a dizzying array of financial information. The manuals which accompany name-band software are usually excellent and will guide you step-by-step into creating a set of books for your company. What's more, all of this computing power is available in software packages costing $200 or less.

Whatever system of accounting you use, it's best to get some professional help from an accountant to set up your books. Accountants can set up the entire system for you, or simply give you advice on whether or not your system satisfies the needs of your business.

WHAT YOU NEED

Manual system To operate a manual system you will need a number of columnar pads of varying widths. A columnar pad is a pad of paper broken down into columns, the most popular being seven columns and fourteen columns. The columnar pads are generally used to summarize similar transactions. For instance, you might summarize **sales** on one and **cheques** on another.

In addition you will need an accounts receivable ledger, accounts payable ledger and a general ledger. These are essentially your books of account. It is within the ledgers and sub-ledgers that vital information about your organization is stored. All of these pads and ledgers are available at most office supply stores. Preparation of manual records is illustrated in chapter 3.

Computerized system If you decide to go the computerized route, you will need one of the accounting software packages designed for small business. The three most popular are:

- Simply Accounting
- Quickbooks
- MYOB Accounting

All of these programs come with considerably more accounting power than a sole proprietor will likely need. They have the capacity to maintain a full array of books and prepare a number of different financial statements and accounting reports. In addition they can print invoices and cheques. Some provide graphs to highlight various aspects of company operations. They are all very user-friendly and designed for those with little accounting expertise.

Since accounting requires very little computer capacity, a high-powered machine isn't essential. You can spend as little as $1,500 to get the basic components of a computer system – monitor, CPU (the processing unit of the computer), keyboard, mouse and printer.

HOW MUCH YOU DO YOURSELF

The issue of how much bookkeeping you should do yourself relates to the specifics of your business. The two main criteria are the availability of your time and your comfort with bookkeeping.

Time is normally scarce when running a small business. Owner-managers are required to wear many hats on a day-to-day basis. You are often responsible for negotiating with customers and suppliers and for ensuring that services are rendered or goods shipped on time. On top of that, you must deal with the bank, the government and the concerns of employees. There is little time left to do the bookkeeping. Furthermore, since bookkeeping is a support function, it tends to take a back seat to the more prominent functions of sales and production. Your entrepreneurial time is often better spent troubleshooting and making sure that the business runs smoothly than entering invoices on the computer or trying to find out why the bank account doesn't balance.

The other criteria is your comfort with bookkeeping. Regardless of how fail-safe an accounting system, its output is only as good as its input. If you enter numerous transactions incorrectly, you may render the books useless. As a famous doctor once said, "It's dangerous to perform brain surgery on yourself."

BOOKKEEPERS AND ACCOUNTANTS

One of the first things to do when starting up a business is to contact an accountant. Accountants can help set up an accounting system and evaluate the reports that are produced. They will review the filing requirements of various government agencies, and assist you in dealing with the bank and other large creditors even if you do most of the basic accounting yourself. Accountants can prepare the year-end financial statements that are submitted to your bank and the taxation authorities. Using professionals in the preparation of your year-end statements give you a twofold advantage:

- They lend additional credibility to the financial statements. (Many users insist that year-end statements be prepared by outside professionals.)
- They can provide valuable management and tax-planning advice about your enterprise. Accountants can be an essential sounding board in making important strategic decisions.

Bookkeepers are individuals who have expertise in record keeping. They can maintain a set of books on a computerized or manual system. They normally don't have the same breadth of expertise as accountants and focus on the more detailed and repetitive aspects of data input.

Since most small businesses don't (in the early stages) require the services of a full-time bookkeeper, many hire a part-time bookkeeper – a self-employed individual who provides services to a variety of small businesses on an hourly basis. Hourly rates vary from $15 to $35. A company doing up to $500,000 of sales a year can probably manage with a bookkeeper five or six days a month, handling input, balancing the bank account and preparing monthly remittances like GST, PST and payroll deductions. Accountants often have contacts with a number of bookkeepers and can refer you to one to assist you in the ongoing maintenance of your books.

Very often small business owners find a hybrid solution to their accounting problem. They do most of the routine bookwork them-selves (assuming they have the time) or have an employee do it, and have a bookkeeper come in monthly to make sure that the books are accurate. There are bookkeepers with considerable com-puter experience who work by the hour and are more than happy to come in a couple of days a month to update the books and pre-pare government remittances.

Get the help you need at startup

Hire the right professionals when starting your business. Too many entrepreneurs are afraid to spend money on good accounting advice at the outset of their business. But any saving on professional fees can easily be squandered by a wasteful or inaccurate system of accounts. (See chapter 13 for more on this.)

CHAPTER TWO

Debits, credits and entries

Accounting reports, including those used in your yearly tax filing, are the product of many individual accounting **entries**. Each reflects a unit of financial information about the business. Businesses function by entering into financial **transactions**. Two of the more common ones are **purchases** and **sales**. Each time a company purchases merchandise from a supplier it is entering into a transaction. Each time a company sells some of its product to a customer it is similarly entering into a transaction. Each of these individual transactions is reflected in the accounting records – in both manual and computer systems – through what are called **entries**. The accounting records in which all the individual entries are reflected are called the **books of account**.

Books of account for most small businesses include a **general ledger**, an **accounts payable ledger**, an **accounts receivable ledger** and perhaps a **sales/cash receipts journal** and a **purchase/cash disbursements journal**. These ledgers and journals provide important information for the day-to-day running of the business, and are the core information from which accounting reports are derived.

Whether you do your books on a computer or in a set of ledger books, you still have to set up a system of accounts to make sense of the money that comes into and goes out from your business.

ACCOUNTS

Accounts are units of information about a company's financial position and operations, representing:

- **assets** – what a company owns and what is owed to the company
- **liabilities** – what a company owes to its creditors
- **revenue** – what a company earns through the sale of its product or services
- **expenses** – what a company has to pay out to earn its revenue

In addition there is a class of accounts called **equity**, which is the net interest that an owner has in the assets of his business. In other words, if a company sold all of its assets and paid all of its debts, what's left would be equity.

Let's use an example of a small business – Moe's Hot Dogs. Moe has a secret recipe for making hot dogs. He has decided to go into manufacturing his hot dogs and incurs several costs in starting up his company. Moe has lent $20,000 to the company, which he is keeping in a bank account. In addition he has acquired a machine for $20,000 with the help of a bank loan. He has not sold anything at this point so he has no revenue or expenses. Moe's company, therefore, has the following account balances:

Assets		Liabilities	
Cash	$20,000	Bank loan	$20,000
Machinery	$20,000		
Total assets	$40,000		
		Equity	
		Owner's advance	$20,000
			$40,000

We can see how the $20,000 loan from Moe has increased the asset account – cash by $20,000. It has also increased the account – owner's advance by $20,000. Owner's advance is an equity account. Equity accounts are affected when owners lend money to their companies. As we mentioned before, equity is the owners' residual interest in the business. If Moe were to sell all his assets and pay off the bank, he would be left with the $20,000 he invested.

The purchase of the machinery for $20,000 was financed by the bank loan. This gave rise to the asset account – machinery and the liability account – bank loan. The books represent a numerical interpretation of the activities of the business.

Let's expand the example to reflect Moe's purchase of supplies for $2,000 and the sale of hot dogs for $3,000. The following two additional accounts and account categories would be brought into existence:

Revenue		
Sales	$3,000	
Expenses		
Supplies	$2,000	

This gives us the basic types of accounts that comprise **accounting ledgers** – assets, liabilities, revenues, expenses and owner's equity. All the accounts that will ever be used in accounting systems fall into one of these five categories. Additional examples of each are:

Assets

Accounts receivable
Investments
Land
Building
Last month's rent
Vehicles

Liabilities

Accounts payable
Bank overdrafts
Term loans

Expenses

Rent
Merchandise purchases
Office expenses
Maintenance
Repairs
Automotive
Professional fees

Equity

Capital stock
Retained earnings
Owner's advances

Revenue

Merchandise sales
Asset sales
Sales of services

13

These are by no means all-inclusive lists. The number and types of accounts you can set up on a computer or in your ledgers can vary as much as the number of different types of businesses in existence. Setting up your books requires many choices pertaining directly to your business. There are certain basic rules to be adhered to, but beyond that, the nature and breakdown of accounts can be as specific as you desire.

Generally each transaction affects at least two accounts. What's more, the amount by which one account is affected must be directly offset by the amount by which another account is affected. Let's use Moe's accounts to illustrate. The initial loan of money to the company from Moe affected *both* the cash account and the owner's advance account. The purchase of machinery affected *both* the machinery account and the bank loan account. In addition, the increase in machinery was directly offset by the increase in the loan account. This reflects the core theory underlying accounting: "double-entry bookkeeping."

DOUBLE-ENTRY BOOKKEEPING

Business transactions are recorded as a combination of debits and credits. As previously mentioned, every transaction affects at least two accounts and a change in one must be offset by a change in the other. The balances in the company accounts at any time are the total debits and credits that have been accumulated through the **posting** of individual entries to the books. There are rules governing which accounts should be debited and which credited in making a journal entry. This is a list of the affects of debits and credits on the different account categories:

Debits	Credits
Increase in assets	Decrease in assets
Decrease in liabilities	Increase in liabilities
Decrease in revenue	Increase in revenue
Increase in expenses	Decrease in expenses
Decrease in equity	Increase in equity

You will note that the two columns appear to be exact opposites of each other – mirror images. This is not a coincidence. Every entry must balance. Debits must always equal credits.

In addition, the books themselves must balance. That is, the total of all the debit accounts must equal all the credit accounts. This system has been in existence for hundreds of years to catch errors, stay on top of bills and keep businesses running smoothly.

A useful way of understanding debits and credits is to see them as sources and uses of financing. Every transaction involves a source and use of funds. Debits almost invariably involve the use of financing and credits provide the source of financing. For instance, the purchase of a car involves the incidence of debt (source of financing – credit) and the acquisition of an asset (use of funds – debit). The company's owners can finance the business in several ways, by borrowing from banks or suppliers, by earning income and by contributions of money. The sources of financing, sales, loans or equity, are all credits whereas the uses of financing, either the acquisition of assets or the incidence of expenses, are debits. We will use this rule to help understand the entries that follow.

Before we go into some examples, let's first clarify the standard classification for the five account categories:

Account Category	Classification
Assets	Debit
Liabilities	Credit
Revenue	Credit
Expenses	Debit
Equity	Credit

This table sets out which account classifications are normally in debit balances and which in credit balances. If a liability account happens to be in a debit balance or an asset account happens to be in a credit balance, this could be an indication that there is an error in the books.

Remember that each business transaction is reflected by a journal entry in the books of account. For example, each time a sale is made it must be entered into the books by a journal entry. Similarly each time a payment of an expense is made, it must be entered.

It's time to return to Moe's, purveyors of wonderful hot dogs.

In Moe's initial transaction, he lent $20,000 to his business. This would affect two accounts, cash and equity. The entry to record this transaction would be:

	Debit	Credit
Cash	$20,000	
Owner's advance		$20,000

When preparing journal entries, remember that debits always appear on the left and credits on the right.

What we can see is the asset account – cash – was increased by $20,000 and the equity account – owner's advance – was increased by a similar $20,000. The increase in assets was directly offset by an increase in liability. The total debits equal the total credits.

Looking at it from an alternative perspective, the owner's advance is a source of financing to the business and therefore a credit. The cash account is a use of financing or a debit.

Cash is the one complication to the rule. When it is increased, it is a use of financing since it had to be increased through either making a sale or borrowing money. When it is decreased, it is a source of financing since cash can be used to pay expenses or acquire assets.

Let's move on to the next transaction in which Moe borrowed $20,000 to acquire machinery. The entry would be:

Machinery	$20,000	
Bank loan		$20,000

In this entry we increased the asset machinery by $20,000 and the liability bank loan by $20,000. Again the debit equals the credit. Again the machinery is a use of financing and therefore a debit and the bank loan is a source of financing and therefore a credit.

Moe then bought himself $2,000 worth of merchandise for resale. We only referred to one side of this transaction before for simplicity, but let's expand it to reflect the fact that Moe used some of his cash to acquire the goods. The entry would be:

| Purchases | $2,000 | | |
| Cash | | $2,000 | |

In this entry we reduced one asset, cash, and increased an expense, purchases. Remember that the reduction of an asset is a credit, much as the increase in a liability is a credit. The increase in the expense was a debit. To again refer to our alternate model, the purchase is a use of financing and therefore a debit, and the cash a source of financing and therefore a credit.

Finally, Moe sold some hot dogs for $3,000. Let's assume he was paid cash. This transaction would be reflected as:

| Cash | $3,000 | | |
| Sales | | $3,000 | |

In this entry we increased cash (asset) by $3,000 and increased sales (revenue) by $3,000. Again the asset was increased by a debit and the revenue increased by a credit – both conform to the table already presented.

In our alternative model, sales provided the financing for the increase in cash and therefore it was a credit, while the increase in cash was the use of financing and therefore a debit.

We now know what transactions are and how they are recorded. We don't, however, know where they are recorded. In the next chapter, we'll look at an actual set of books.

CAPITAL ASSETS AND AMORTIZATION

Capital assets are assets that have a useful life of over one year. For most small businesses they include: machinery and equipment, furniture and fixtures and automotive equipment. These assets are used up in earning income over a period of time. A major decision in recording transactions is whether a particular expenditure should be **capitalized** or **written off**. Expenditures are capitalized when the asset acquired is of enduring value – it has a useful life that

17

extends beyond the current year. For instance, the machinery that makes Moe's hot dogs would be capitalized and amortized over its useful life. Expenditures are written off, or charged to income, if they are used up prior to the end of the current year. The meat Moe uses would be written off, since it is entirely used up within a few days.

Assets are considered to be consumed in earning income. Regardless of whether they are used up in one year or over a number of years, a portion of their economic value is consumed as your company earns income. **Amortization** is the manner in which capital assets are written off over their useful lives.

Let's take the example of Moe's. Moe acquired machinery for $20,000 with a loan in January of his first year. Say the machinery has a useful life of 10 years. Depreciation of the machinery would be recorded as:

Depreciation expense	$2,000		
Machinery		$2,000	

This entry reduces the accounting value of the machinery after taking into account the portion that has been used up in earning income. We have reduced the asset account and increased the expense account by the amount of the depreciation.

GLOSSARY

Transaction A business occurrence measured in monetary terms (a payment or a deposit).

Entry The manner in which transactions are recorded in the accounting records.

Accounting records The records of a company's financial activities, including its books of account, supporting invoices, cheques, contracts and deposit slips.

Supporting documentation The source documents that support a transaction – cheques, invoices, bank statements, etc.

Account An account groups information about a class of items – sales, office expenses, travel, etc.

Assets Whatever a company owns that has value. These could be cash in the bank, outstanding accounts with customers (accounts receivable), machinery and equipment, even good will.

Liabilities What a company owes – the debts to its creditors. These could be bank loans, outstanding accounts with suppliers (accounts payable), unpaid government remittances.

Revenues The amount a company earns in selling a product or rendering a service. Examples of revenues are sales, fees earned, interest income.

Expenses The amount a company incurs in selling its product or service. Examples of expenses are rent, salaries and wages, purchases of merchandise for resale.

Equity The net financial interest in an enterprise of its owners (what's left after you sell the assets and pay the liabilities).

Books of account The financial records that are the product of the company's accounting system, including the general ledger, the various journals, the subsidiary ledgers.

General ledger The financial record in which the accounts summarizing the company's financial position and results of operations are maintained. This is where the balances of the various assets, liabilities, revenue and expenses can be found.

Accounts payable The amount owing to a company's creditors.

Accounts receivable The amount due from a company's customers.

Accounts payable subsidiary ledger A record showing a breakdown of the amount owing to each individual supplier. It is normally balanced with the accounts payable figure in the general ledger, which is a total of all accounts payable owing.

Accounts receivable subsidiary ledger A record showing a breakdown of the amount owing from each individual customer. It is normally balanced with the accounts receivable figure in the general ledger, which is the total of all accounts receivable due.

Balance sheet A financial report detailing a company's financial position at a certain point in time.

Income statement A financial report showing the results of a company's operations for a certain period of time.

Journals Tools for summarizing transactions of a similar nature. Examples are purchase journal, accounts payable journal, accounts receivable journal, sales journal.

Set up accounts that suit your business

Revenue Canada has a suggested format on the T2124 statement of business income, but these categories may or may not meet the needs of your business. For instance, you might want to reflect income from two or more sources on your statement rather than the one category available on the T2124. Similarly, the breakdown of expenses as provided on the form may not adequately reflect the financial reality of your business. You may have certain types of expenses that the government has not considered essential to *their* understanding of your accounts. But they may be of considerable interest to you.

So when you set up your accounts, make sure the categories reflect the information that you need, not just what's convenient for the government.

CHAPTER THREE

Ledgers and journals – your set of books

Let's look at how transactions are recorded in the **books of account**. We previously mentioned that it is easier to understand the recording of information in manually prepared accounting records, so we'll use the manual model to explain bookkeeping. Computerized systems record transactions in the same way as manual systems, but the flow of information to the various ledgers is usually automatic. While computers make the accounting easy, let's review the basic ideas in a manual system to help you understand how accounting information is handled.

GENERAL LEDGER

The general ledger is your main source of information about the assets, liabilities, equity, revenue and expenses of your small business. It is within the general ledger that all of the individual entries are posted and account balances are accumulated. Each major financial item is represented by a separate general ledger account. All transactions relating to that item are recorded via journal entry and accumulated over the accounting period.

Before the advent of computers, each account was represented by a page in a binder on which all related transactions were posted. With computers, printouts break down transactions by account, but transactions relating to several accounts may appear on the same page. Regardless, the general ledger is the record that is the primary source of information about your company's financial position and results of operations. It is from the general ledger that you derive the income statement, balance sheet and statement of cash flow for your business.

Let's carry on with Moe's Hot Dogs. The accounts that we are setting up here are not all-inclusive, but relate solely to those transactions and journal entries mentioned so far:

Account	Debit	Credit	Balance in account	
			Debit	Credit
Cash				
Entry 1 Moe's capital contributions	$20,000		$20,000	
Entry 3 Purchase of merchandise		$2,000	$18,000	
Entry 4 Sale of merchandise	$3,000		$21,000	
Machinery				
Entry 2 To record the purchase of machinery	$20,000		$20,000	
Entry 5 To record depreciation		$2,000	$18,000	
Bank loan				
Entry 2 To record the purchase of machinery		$20,000		$20,000
Equity				
Entry 1 To record Moe's capital contribution		$20,000		$20,000
Sales				
Entry 4 To record the sale of merchandise		$3,000		$3,000
Purchases				
Entry 3 To record the purchase of merchandise	$2,000		$2,000	
Depreciation expense				
Entry 5 To record depreciation	$2,000		$2,000	

We have now posted all of the entries to our general ledger. Once we have posted our general ledger, the next thing to do in a manual system is prepare a **trial balance**.

 A trial balance is relevant only when using a manual system. In fact the whole idea of posting is now obsolete for those using computers since all computer programs post entries automatically to all relevant accounts in the general ledger. In addition, the books are automatically balanced each time a journal entry is recorded.

The trial balance is run to ensure that the books are in balance after the posting. This is also a way to be certain that the entries were recorded correctly since an out-of-balance condition could relate to an improperly recorded journal entry. Since the debits and credits must be equal in each individual entry, they must by extension be equal in the entire general ledger.

Let's have a look at Moe's trial balance:

Account	Debit	Credit
Cash	$21,000	
Machinery	$18,000	
Bank loan		$20,000
Equity		$20,000
Sales		$3,000
Purchases	$2,000	
Depreciation	$2,000	
Total	$43,000	$43,000

Moe can now be comfortable that his journal entries were recorded accurately in the accounts.

JOURNALS

The journals are yet another element of the accounting system that has been rendered more or less obsolete with the advent of computers. Again, a thorough understanding of a manual system will provide a better insight into the buildup and interrelationship of the accounting numbers.

As you have probably discovered from the preceding illustration, recording each transaction by journal entry and then posting it to the general ledger would make the accounting process far too cumbersome and time-consuming. To reduce this tedium and duplication, the use of journals was implemented. The accounting journals summarize similar transactions, say cash disbursements or receipts, and post them to the general ledger only once monthly rather than each time a transaction occurs.

Let's use three different types of journals to post Moe's transactions:

1. sales/cash receipts journal
2. purchase/cash disbursement journal
3. general journal

The first two journals are for recurring transactions that can be summarized easily. The general journal is for non-recurring transactions that don't lend themselves to summarizing.

Sales/cash receipts journal Individual sales invoices are generally recorded identically. Since the same accounts are debited and credited, the only difference between recording individual invoices is the amount. (We are assuming here that sales are not made on credit, and are settled in cash upon delivery of the goods. This is a simplified model for the purposes of explanation, since most wholesale trade is conducted on credit.)

Now let's assume that Moe has 50 hot dog sales a month, rather than the one he has made. It is obvious that posting each entry individually would be prohibitively tedious. Journals allow Moe to summarize his entries and make one posting to the general ledger instead of 50. Moe will summarize similar transactions by listing them on a columnar pad, adding up the columns and preparing one journal entry for the total.

Let's look at three separate invoices, summarize them and prepare the entry:

Customer	Invoice No.	Cash	Sales	
Joe's Restaurant	1	$2,500	$2,500	
Max's Eatery	2	$1,500	$1,500	
Laury's Luncheonette	3	$1,000	$1,000	
		$5,000	$5,000	

The journal entry to record the above three invoices would be:

Cash	$5,000		
Sales		$5,000	

This one entry summarizes the three that would otherwise be made in the general ledger. In addition, the journal provides the opportunity to record other details of the transaction. Full details of each transaction normally do not appear in the general ledger since it would get too cluttered.

Purchase/cash disbursement journal The purchase/cash disbursement journal is similar to the sales/cash journal, but is used to summarize amounts paid rather than amounts received. This journal generally requires many more columns than the cash receipt/sales journal owing to the fact that a small business normally receives money for only a few reasons, but spends money for many different reasons. For example, money will come into a small business as a loan from a bank, an advance for the owner or a sale of merchandise. On the other hand, money will go out of a business for many more reasons: to buy merchandise for resale, to buy office supplies or new equipment, to pay car expenses, salaries or rent, to name a few. It is for this reason that a 14-column pad is better for writing up a cash disbursement journal. Seven columns will suffice in writing up cash receipts.

Let's look at four different transactions of this type. The first two relate to buying merchandise for resale, the third relates to payment of a salary and the fourth relates to payment of rent.

Moe bought $1,500 worth of supplies form Saul's Emporium. He then went on to buy some seasoning from Spicy Max's for

$2,000. He paid the rent of $1,000 to Lou's Properties and paid his employee Alfred $250 for the first week of work.

Now let's assume that Moe summarizes these entries with the help of a cash disbursement journal.

Payee	Cheque	Amount	Purchases	Rent	Salaries
Saul's Emporium	1	$1,500	$1,500		
Spicy Max's	2	$2,000	$2,000		
Lou's Properties	3	$1,000		$1,000	
Alfred	4	$250			$250
		$4,750	$3,500	$1,000	$250

The summarized entry would be:

Purchases	$3,500	
Rent	$1,000	
Wages	$250	
Cash		$4,750

General journal As we mentioned previously, the general journal is used for transactions of a non-recurring or unusual nature. A good example of one of these is called a **reallocation**. This type of entry is prepared either when an amount is erroneously posted to the wrong account or when year-end procedures require the recording of certain types of entries like depreciation.

An example of the correction of an error would go like this: Let's assume that Moe bought a car for $10,000, but he erroneously allocated the purchase to his purchases account. The entry to correct this would be:

Vehicles	$10,000	
Purchases		$10,000

With this entry Moe has increased his asset account – vehicles and reduced the expense account – purchases. One can see how this entry is neither a cash disbursement or cash receipt and would, therefore, not be appropriately included in either of the preceding journals.

WHAT YOU REALLY NEED

For many very small businesses, the journals are all the owner-manager really need prepare. Maintaining a full set of books can be terribly time-consuming and distract attention from more important tasks. Listing deposits and disbursements will certainly give the entrepreneur some idea about the revenues he is earning and the expenses incurred. They will also, with minor modification, enable the calculation of monthly or quarterly sales tax remittances. A bookkeeper can then be hired to post the entries to a general ledger at month-end. Alternatively, you could wait until year-end and then give the summaries to an accountant. Although these records are not comprehensive, they are certainly helpful to any professional and will ultimately cut down on the accounting fees you'll be charged.

Computerized systems When computers are used, summaries often become redundant. Computer software is designed to post *all* transactions to the general ledger automatically. What's more, most programs do not accept out-of-balance entries so it is virtually impossible that books be out-of-balance.

Programs generally post full details of each transaction to the general ledger. What this means is that each general ledger account will not only contain a reference to a cash disbursement page or a journal entry, but will contain full details of the payee or payer. This is why entries generally appear at three different places in computerized books. Each entry is reflected in the system's general journal as well as in all accounts affected.

Let's go back to the first two purchase transactions referred to above – the purchase from Saul's and Spicy Max's. If Moe used a computerized system, something like this would appear in his general ledger accounts:

The details that are available in the summary in the manual system are now fully reproduced in the computerized general ledger. What's more, each transaction is fully described twice in the general ledger, once on the debit side and once on the credit side. General ledgers in computerized systems tend to be crammed with information and may contain hundreds of pages of data, even for a very small business. For that reason these particular reports are not run very frequently unless you plan to rent a separate office to store paper.

SUBSIDIARY LEDGERS

In the examples we have used so far, all transactions were settled in cash. Sales of merchandise and purchases of supplies were both paid COD. This is a convenient way to learn accounting but is rarely indicative of the way business is conducted. Anyone in a wholesale or service business certainly has a large number of credit transactions, both on the revenue and on the expense side. If you are in a retail business, either a store or a restaurant, services and merchandise are generally sold COD – but in almost all cases, credit is required with company suppliers. Subsidiary ledgers are a necessary component of your records if you engage in a large number of credit transactions.

Sales on Credit

Previously we recorded Moe's sales as:

Cash	$5,000		
Sales		$5,000	

As the sale was made, the cash was collected. But with credit sales we have an intermediate step – the creation of **accounts receivable**. Accounts receivable are those debts owed to you by your customers. They are an asset of your company, just like cash or equipment. In fact, they are a highly desirable asset since they generally will be converted to cash over the near term.

Let's say that Moe's Hot Dogs sold some merchandise to Gerry's Hot Feet, a dance club in the area.

Gerry said that he required 30-day terms from Moe. He bought $5,000 worth of hot dogs on credit. The entry would be:

Accounts receivable	$5,000		
Sales		$5,000	

At the end of 30 days, Gerry paid for the hot dogs. The entry would be recorded:

Cash	$5,000		
Accounts receivable		$5,000	

During the period that the $5,000 was outstanding, Moe had to keep track of it. If he forgot about his receivable, he would run the risk of losing control of who owed him money. Assuming that Moe develops many customers like Gerry, the risk of losing track of the outstanding receivables is considerable. The general ledger would be of no help since it only presents a global number of all the receivables outstanding, but does not provide a breakdown by customer. It is for this reason that the **accounts receivable subsidiary ledger** was invented – to break down the total figure in the general ledger by individual customer and provide historical information on a customer-by-customer basis. This way, after a year or so, Moe will know which customers pay on time and which are deadbeats.

Accounts receivable subsidiary ledger How is information recorded on the subsidiary ledger? The answer is: each transaction has to be posted to the general and subsidiary ledgers (unless you use a computer – which does the two at once). The operative concept here is that the transactions must be recorded in two places. Despite the tedium, there really is no way around it for a company with a large number of accounts receivable.

Moe only has one customer at this point, so his subsidiary ledger will comprise that one account. The terms "account" and "customer" are used interchangeably when it comes to the subsidiary ledger. Each customer has his own ledger account, or page, in the subsidiary ledger. Each ledger page contains information on invoices charged to that customer and payments made by that customer.

Let's take a look at the subsidiary ledger page for Gerry's Hot Feet:

Gerry's Hot Feet

Reference (Inv #, chq #)	Date	Invoice	Payment	Opening Balance	Closing Balance
# 1	May 10	$5,000			$5,000
(Chq #?)	June 10		$5,000	$5,000	nil

The added detail provides additional support for the entry if there is a dispute with the customer or in the event of a government audit. Note that the subsidiary ledger must always be in agreement with the general ledger. If an out-of-balance condition exists, it could mean that an invoice or payment went unrecorded and the accounts receivable records are inaccurate. What is called an accounts receivable trial balance should be prepared regularly. Make sure that the total of the individual sub-ledger accounts is equal to the balance of the general ledger account.

Accounts payable subsidiary ledger Many small businesses have credit arrangements with at least some of their suppliers. To keep track of the balances owing to each supplier, an accounts payable subsidiary ledger is necessary.

The accounting for accounts receivable and accounts payable is strikingly similar. In fact, they are mirror images of each other. You are the customer in the accounts receivable records of those suppliers whose accounts you maintain in your accounts payable records.

Let's take an example of the type of entry giving rise to accounts payable, record the payment of the outstanding balance and show how the payable entry is reflected in the subsidiary ledger. Of course at this point you understand that all journal entries are automatically posted to the general ledger, either as part of a summary (journal) or individually.

Moe has negotiated credit terms with Blacky's Slaughterhouse. He has acquired $12,000 worth of beef on account, which is to be paid within 60 days. The first general ledger entry reflects the purchase of the beef and the second the payment of the outstanding balance:

Purchases	$12,000		
Accounts payable		$12,000	

To record the purchase of beef

Accounts payable	$12,000		
Cash		$12,000	

To record the payment of the balance owing

Moe's accounts payable subsidiary ledger account for Blacky's Slaughterhouse would reflect the following:

Blacky's Slaughterhouse

Reference	Date	Payment	Bill	Balance
125	June 10		$12,000	$12,000
5	August 10	$12,000		nil

Again you can see how complete details of the transaction are recorded. The debits and credits to the accounts payable subsidiary ledger accounts are identical to the debits and credits to the general ledger account. As is the case with the receivable sub-ledger, a periodic trial balance of the subsidiary ledger accounts should be prepared.

Computerized payable and receivable systems
Most computer programs segregate information processing into what are called modules. Generally the modules would be referred to as accounts payable, accounts receivable and general ledger. Transactions would be inputted to the module corresponding to their type. For instance, purchase transactions would be inputted through the accounts payable module and sales would be inputted through the accounts receivable module. General journal entries would be inputted through the general ledger module.

As mentioned earlier, different transactions might need to be posted in more than one set of records, particularly if they give rise to accounts receivable or accounts payable. The reason for this is that additional information is required on outstanding payables and receivables so that bills can be paid and sales collected. Computers don't know ahead of time which particular records need to be updated upon inputting a transaction. The computer effectively has to be told whether or not a certain transaction has to be entered on a subsidiary ledger. This information is provided when the transaction is processed through the appropriate module.

For instance, to ensure that sales transactions are appropriately posted to the accounts receivable subsidiary ledger, they would have to be recorded through the accounts receivable module.

Of course, all transactions have to be recorded to the general ledger, but not all general ledger transactions have to be posted to subsidiary ledgers. Any transaction input to a subsidiary ledger through either the accounts receivable or accounts payable module on a computer is automatically posted to the general ledger. This is a principal advantage of using a computerized system. Not only is the general ledger automatically balanced upon inputting each individual entry, but all of the subsidiary ledgers are balanced with their related general ledger accounts.

Alternatives to the subsidiary ledger system Although there is no way around the subsidiary ledger system for those with a large number of accounts receivable and accounts payable, for smaller businesses with a lower volume of transactions other alternatives are available.

For instance, you might just keep an open invoice file. Keeping unpaid accounts receivable and unpaid accounts payable in file folders accomplishes this. At any given time, the total of unpaid items will simply be the total of invoices in the folder. When items are paid, they simply get moved from the unpaid folder to a paid file.

Another alternative would be to maintain an informal list of open items. When the items are paid, the list need merely be updated. This could be done weekly or monthly. If several items per customer or supplier are open simultaneously, this system may not be affective. The objective of any payable or receivable system is the maintenance of accurate and complete records. If too many corners are cut in the name of brevity, the resulting accounting information may be useless.

Recording transactions by computer

Computer programs record and input information by module. Just as similar transactions are summarized in a manual system, similar transactions are recorded through the applicable module in the computer system.

Module	Transactions recorded	Documents and reports prepared
Sales/accounts receivable	Sales Cash receipts	Invoices Client statements Accounts receivable aged listings
Purchases/accounts payable	Purchases Payments	Accounts payable aged listing Cheques
General ledger	Miscellaneous journal entries	General journal Trial balance Income statement Balance sheet
Payroll	Salaries	Paycheques Monthly remittances Annual T4s and summaries

CHAPTER FOUR

Your financial reports

The ledgers and journals in the preceding chapter provide the raw material from which your financial reports are prepared. Your financial reports are critical to the management of your business both from a long-term and short-term perspective. For the short term, they provide much-needed information on the financial requirements of your business; for the long term, they provide essential information for plotting strategy to achieve future goals.

ACCOUNTS RECEIVABLE AGED LISTING

The accounts receivable aged listing is a list of unpaid sales invoices broken down by customer and the "age" of the bill. It is produced directly from information obtained from the accounts receivable subsidiary ledger. The list is used for these purposes:

- It allows you to estimate cash flow. A careful review of the list provides information on how much cash you can anticipate collecting in the near term.

- It provides evidence of the accuracy of the accounting system. If the list of unpaid invoices appears to be out of line, chances are there were errors in its compilation. These could relate to weaknesses in other aspects of the accounting system that have to be addressed.

- Since invoices are summarized by age (30 days, 60 days, 90 days), it provides you with a necessary tool in controlling credit limits and sales. It provides information on whether customers are staying within their credit limits and whether they are paying their invoices promptly. It therefore affects future credit decisions.

- It also provides your bank with necessary information on monitoring your company's bank loan. Accounts receivable are often pledged to the bank as security for bank debts. The bank generally requires an aged listing of accounts receivable on a monthly basis.

To see what this report looks like let's go back to our old friend Moe. It's now the end of Moe's first year in business. He has five customers with outstanding balances in his subsidiary ledger:

Moe's Hot Dogs
Accounts Receivable Listing
December 31

Customer Name	Amount Due	Current	(Days Old)			
			30	60	90	Over 90
Manny's Delicatessan	$550	$550				
Max's Restaurant	$750		$750			
Gerry's Hot Feet	$2,000			$2,000		
Ralph's Fine Foods	$4,500				$4,500	
Larry's Watering Hole	$1,800					$1,800
Total	$9,600	$550	$750	$2,000	$4,500	$1,800

Apparently, Moe has been a little lax in administering his accounts receivable. Although only one of his accounts is over 90 days old, this is about 20 percent of the total outstanding. In addition, only $550 is in the current column. It is essential for startup entrepreneurs not to let their accounts receivable get too far out of line. Remember the older an account gets the more difficult it becomes to collect.

Running a business almost always requires setting up a line of credit with a bank. A line of credit is a loan that fluctuates on a day-to-day basis depending on a business's needs. Certainly if you are going to be carrying a considerable amount of accounts receivable you should set up some form of credit arrangement with a bank.

The reason for this is that suppliers of new business normally require payment on a COD basis. This could easily cause a cash squeeze if you are not forthcoming with payment.

Banks will margin accounts receivable, which means that they will provide loans of up to a certain percentage of current accounts receivable. Their general policy is to finance 67 percent of accounts receivable that are less than 60 days old. If you want to advance credit to customers in excess of 60 days, you're on your own. This is certainly another reason to stay on top of your accounts receivable. Our friend Moe is in some trouble owing to the relatively small percentage of his accounts receivable that fall within the bank's lending criteria. He would be limited to a bank loan of 67 percent of $3300. Any accounts receivable in excess of that will have to be financed by Moe himself.

ACCOUNTS PAYABLE LISTING

The accounts payable listing is the equivalent of the receivable listing. It provides you with helpful information.

- It helps you plan your cash requirements over the near term by informing management of what amounts will have to be paid over the coming period.
- It provides evidence about the accuracy of your accounting system. Again, amounts that appear unreasonable could be evidence of errors in the system.
- It could provide evidence of the overall financial health of your business. Accounts payable that increase without a commensurate increase in sales could mean declining financial strength.

 Make it a point to study your accounts payable and accounts receivable listings on a regular basis. This will help you monitor the health of your company and the accuracy of your accounting. It will also give you a sense of near-term cash requirements.

Here is an aged listing of Moe's accounts payable at December 31:

Supplier Name	Amount	Current	30	60	90	Over 90
Blacky's Slaughterhouse	$2,500	$2,500				
Saul's Emporium	$1,500			$1,500		
Spicey Max's	$1,800		$1,800			
Lundrake Hydro	$1,200				$1,200	
Alberta Wholesale Gas	$850					$850
Total	$7,850	$2,500	$1,800	$1,500	$1,200	$850

As we can see, Moe can count on being called by Alberta Wholesale Gas in the near term. In addition he is perilously close to getting his power cut off. Moe should be paying more attention to his financial reports.

FINANCIAL STATEMENTS

The financial statements provide critical information about your small business, its financial condition and the results of its operations – whether or not it is earning money. For a large business, financial statements are complex documents requiring professional assistance in their preparation. Nonetheless, a person running a small business with billing below $200,000 a year should be able to do most, if not all, of the necessary accounting. A computer program will certainly help, but we'll begin our explanation with a manual system for clarity. The illustrations provided here are necessarily simplified.

The starting point in extracting the information for a set of financial statements is to prepare the general ledger trial balance illustrated in chapter 3. We will provide a more comprehensive example of a trial balance here as a starting point in extracting the information for our financial statements:

Moe's Hot Dogs
Trial Balance
For the year ended December 31

	Debit	Credit	
Cash	$24,250		
Accounts receivable	$9,600		
Equipment	$18,000		
Accounts payable		$7,850	
Bank loan		$20,000	
Owner's advance		$20,000	
Sales		$50,000	
Purchases	$15,000		
Rent	$5,000		
Salaries	$12,000		
Utilities	$7,000		
Legal and accounting	$3,000		
Depreciation	$2,000		
Repairs and maintenance	$2,000		
	$97,850	$97,850	

There are several points worth noting here:

- The general ledger account balances from which the trial balance was prepared resulted from many different journal entries throughout the year. We have not shown all of the entries owing to space constraints.
- Both the accounts receivable and the accounts payable figures in the general ledger trial balance tie into the totals of the accounts receivable and accounts payable previously displayed.
- All of the information required to prepare the financial statements is in the general ledger; it just needs to be reformatted.

Computerized trial balances Computers have done away with balancing. As we mentioned previously each individual transaction entered into a computer automatically updates all relevant accounting records. For instance, a sales invoice will automatically update the appropriate general and subsidiary ledger accounts. In so doing, the books are always in balance. A trial balance can be run after every transaction is inputted.

Income Statement Once you have prepared the trial balance, you can prepare an income statement by simply extracting the revenue and expense accounts. With the income statement you know if your business is making or losing money, and also whether your expenses are reasonable given the level of sales.

Let's take a look at Moe's results for the year:

Moe's Hot Dogs
Income Statement
For the year ended December 31

Income
Sales	<u>$50,000</u>

Cost of sales
Purchases	$15,000
Salaries and wages	<u>$12,000</u>
	<u>$27,000</u>

Gross profit <u>$23,000</u>

Overhead
Rent	$5,000
Utilities	$7,000
Legal and accounting	$3,000
Repairs and maintenance	$2,000
Depreciation	<u>$2,000</u>
	<u>$19,000</u>

Net income for the year <u>$4,000</u>

We can prepare Moe's income statement simply by taking the information straight off the trial balance. Income statements are customarily displayed as follows:

1. The first item is the revenue of the business.
2. The next items are those related to the cost of sales. These are expenses that vary directly with the level of sales. Generally they include goods purchased for resale, wages, commission, freight and anything else involved in purchase or manufacture of goods for resale.
3. The next item shown is the gross profit. This amount represents the profit left after the cost of items acquired or produced for resale are deducted.
4. Following the cost of sales and gross profit are the overhead items. These are the miscellaneous items of running a business and are generally not directly related to the volume of sales. For instance, rent is normally a fixed cost that does not vary regardless of the level of a company's sales.
5. The final item is the net income. This is the profit left to the company after the deduction of all its expenses. The net income figure is used in the calculation of your **income taxes**. Revenue Canada will rarely accept your **accounting income** as an indication of the company's **taxable income** however. In fact, good accounting measurement and taxation policy are sometimes at odds (see chapter 5).

Closing the books The procedure of closing the books involves reducing all of the revenue and expense accounts in the general ledger to zero and transferring the **net** result to the shareholders' **equity** account. The effect of this is to transfer the net income over to the balance sheet portion of the general ledger. The equity account becomes the final resting place of the difference between the revenue and expense accounts for the year.

Confused? Let's prepare Moe's closing entries:

Moe's Hot Dogs
Closing Entry
December 31

	Debit	Credit	
Sales	$50,000		
Purchases		$15,000	
Rent		$5,000	
Salaries		$12,000	
Utilities		$7,000	
Legal and accounting		$3,000	
Repairs and maintenance		$2,000	
Depreciation		$2,000	
Retained income		$4,000	
Total	$50,000	$50,000	

Effectively what we have done in closing the books is transferred the net income of the business to Moe's retained income account (retained income is an equity account). Remember that the net income is merely the net difference determined when expense accounts (debits) are deducted from revenue accounts (credits). This makes sense for a number of reasons:

- We noted earlier that an increase in equity is a credit. When a company earns money it increases the owner's interest in the business. In Moe's case, his interest in the assets of the business was increased by $4,000. If the company lost money, then the owner's interest in the assets of the business would have been reduced. This would have been reflected as a debit, or a decrease, in Moe's equity.
- We noted earlier that a credit could be viewed alternatively as an increase in financing. One of the principal ways that businesses finance themselves is through the process of earning income. As income is earned, the company's financial position strengthens. In this particular case the credit to owner capital of $4,000 represents a source of financing the business has acquired through running profitably.

Balance sheet Now that we have prepared the income statement and discussed how the income statement ties into the balance sheet, we are ready to prepare the balance sheet for Moe's Hot Dogs. Balance sheets are normally extracted from the trial balance in much the same way income statements are. One major adjustment is the addition of net income or deduction of net loss from the equity accounts.

Balance sheets are usually set up like this:

• Assets are on the left-hand side (asset accounts should always be in a debit position).

• Liabilities and equities are on the right-hand side (liabilities should always be in a credit position). Equities may be in a debit position if a company has accumulated losses. These are still shown on the right-hand side but are shown as a deduction.

• Assets are broken down between current and long term. Generally, needed information is provided if the users of financial statements can determine what assets will be converted to cash within the coming year.

• Liabilities are broken down into current and long term. Needed information is provided to financial statement users if they can determine what debts will become due within one year.

• Equities are separated prominently from liabilities. Users of financial statements want to know how much of the operation is financed internally versus the portion that is financed with the help of loans or other outside sources.

• Balance sheets reflect information at a certain point in time rather than over a period of time. The balance sheet shows what the financial position of the company is at the date it is prepared. Income statements reflect the results of the operation over a time span.

Let's now look at Moe's balance sheet:

Moe's Hot Dogs
Balance Sheet
As at December 31

ASSETS			LIABILITIES	
Current			**Current**	
Cash	$24,250		Accounts payable	$7,850
Accounts receivable	$9,600			
Total current assets	$33,850			
Long-term assets			**Long term**	
Equipment	$18,000		Bank loan	$20,000
			Total liabilities	$27,850
			EQUITY	
			Owner's advance	$20,000
			Retained income	$4,000
				$24,000
Total assets	$51,850		**Total liabilities**	$51,850

CHAPTER FIVE

Paying your taxes

WHAT IS TAXABLE INCOME?

Income tax is levied on a company's taxable income. As a starting point you should understand the difference between **accounting** income and **taxable** income. Accounting income is the amount that is determined by deducting your expenses from revenue. The revenue and expenses are extracted from your books after the completion of an accounting period. All expenses incurred are deducted in the calculation of accounting income. Some of these expenses may not be **allowable** for income tax purposes, however.

Allowable expenses are those that the government permits the company to deduct in arriving at its taxable income. The deductibility of expenses is determined with reference to:

Reasonableness of an expense In the absence of specific rules disallowing a certain type of deduction, the main criteria in assessing the deductibility of an expense is its reasonableness – was it incurred to earn income? For instance, an owner of a business may insist that it is necessary to maintain a condo in Hawaii to entertain customers, while the government might take a different position. Although the expense reduced accounting income, it may not be allowable as a deduction in arriving at taxable income.

Public policy This is far more arbitrary and relates to the government's priorities in encouraging certain types of expenditures. An example of this type of deduction is the write-off of computer equipment for those involved in research and development. Even though a computer is an asset of enduring value, which would normally appear on the balance sheet, the government allows the full cost of computer equipment to be written off in the year acquired.

Perceived abuse The government will arbitrarily disallow certain types of expenses simply because they fear that the deduction is being abused. An example of this is the limitation on the deductibility of club fees. You may consider it absolutely essential to be a member of a certain club in order to attract business, so you deduct the fees on your income statement. Unfortunately, the income tax rules regarding club fees prohibit their deduction regardless of the circumstances.

 Financial statements are normally not prepared solely for taxation purposes; they are prepared as a window on your business. They provide you and others with meaningful information on how your company is doing so that credit and management decisions can be made. It is risky to prepare a statement solely for income tax purposes since this could distort the operating results. Expenses deducted in the calculation of net income should be those **incurred** not necessarily **tax deductible**.

EXPENSES TO BE WARY OF

There are certain types of expenses that the government pays specific attention to in the calculation of your company's taxable income. These are expenses that are either completely or partially disallowed, or subject to government enforced restrictions. Here are some of the more significant ones:

Meals and entertainment The government scrutinizes meals and entertainment expenses closely; 50 percent of these are disallowed for tax purposes, the theory being – you were going to have to eat anyway, so why allow you to deduct your own meal? Even though there may be more than three people attending the meal, the deduction is restricted to 50 percent of the total bill.

Donations Donations are not considered expenses of running a business in all but the most unusual situations. They are considered acts of charity. Even though business owners are often asked by their customers to make charitable contributions, the contribution would not be considered a business expense. It may be deductible, but its deductibility is governed by the rules governing charitable donations, not business expenses.

Vehicle expenses Vehicle expenses include capital cost allowance, insurance, gas and oil, repairs and maintenance, licenses and are limited to the portion of the mileage that can be attributed directly to the business. The government has taken to requiring a mileage log to substantiate business mileage. (A mileage log is a book in which you list all your business trips daily.)

Home office expenses The dramatic increase in consulting businesses run out of private residences across the country has focused Revenue Canada's attention on home office expenses.

Several rules have been implemented regarding the deduction of home office rent. These are:

- The portion of the home used as an office must not have alternate uses. If the kid's playroom has a desk in it, this may not qualify as an office.
- That customers or clients actually visit the home office. If it is an official place of business, then you must be prepared to see customers there.
- That home office expenses may not be used to create or increase a loss from a business. If your business lost money in a particular year prior to claiming a deduction for home office rent, no home office rent deduction may be claimed. (The expenses could be carried forward to use in a following year however.)

Capital cost allowance (CCA) This is the income tax version of depreciation. There are rates of CCA that Revenue Canada allows for particular capital assets (which may or may not have some connection to an asset's useful life). Assets are grouped into classes and each class is assigned a rate of CCA. For instance, machinery and equipment is one class and automotive equipment another. The rate for machinery is 20 percent and for automotive, 30 percent. This means that 20 percent of the remaining undepreciated balance of your machinery and 30 percent of the undepreciated balance of your automotive equipment can be claimed in the year.

Amortization vs. capital cost allowance As we previously mentioned, amortization is the manner in which capital assets are charged to income. It should be based on an estimate of the asset's useful life to provide a useful measure of the amount of the asset used up in earning income. It is not recognized as a tax-deductible expense.

RECONCILING ACCOUNTING AND TAXABLE INCOME

Revenue Canada provides several ways of calculating your taxable small business income:

- One is with the aid of a T2124 Statement of Business Activities. This is simply an income statement prepared in the format preferred by Revenue Canada. It closely parallels your income statement, but excludes non-deductible expenses and includes support for the business portion of vehicle, home office and meal and entertainment expenses. If you wish to use this form, you must transfer the figures appearing on your income statement to the Revenue Canada format.
- The other is with the aid of T2130 Reconciliation of Net Income (Business). This provides a space for your accounting income, and then lists those items that differ in the calculation of taxable income. When you use the T2130 form, you include a copy of your company's financial statements.

Let's say that our friend Moe is about to prepare his tax return. His taxable income is $4,000. He has deducted club dues of $2,000 and meals and entertainment expenses of $1,500 on his income statement. The following would appear on his T2130 form:

Net income per financial statements	$4,000
Add:	
Club dues	$2,000
Meals and entertainment x 50%	$750
Taxable income	$6,750

GST

In 1991 the government brought in a national sales tax. All goods and services sold in Canada are subject to GST with the following exceptions:

- **Bank charges and interest**
- **Insurance**
- **Medical and dental expenses**
- **Groceries**
- **Exported goods and services**

In addition, to avoid some of the bookkeeping complexity that comes with having to collect and remit GST, the government has provided an exemption for very small businesses selling less than $30,000 of taxable goods or services.

GST, like any other sales tax, is simply a charge on your invoice. Assuming that Moe sold some hot dogs out of province (so no PST would be billed) Moe's invoice for 500 hot dogs would be:

Moe's
Hot Dogs

May 31, 2000

Gerry's Hot Feet
25 Longtoe Blvd.
Massapicki

For supply of 500 hot dogs	$250.00
GST 7% (No.000000000)	17.50
Amount due:	$267.50

If Gerry does not pay COD, the entry to record the invoice would be:

Accounts receivable	$267.50		
Sales		$250.00	
GST		$17.50	

The accounts receivable is set up for the full amount since Gerry is responsible to pay the GST. Moe records a sale of only $250 however, the balance being a liability for $17.50, the amount that Moe has billed Gerry in trust for the government. It, therefore, becomes a debt of Moe's business. If Gerry fails to pay the accounts receivable, however, Moe can subsequently reduce his GST liability for the uncollectible amount.

GST paid Your small business is only liable to remit the difference between the GST collected and the GST paid to the government. For this reason, it is essential that your accounting system compile all of the required information. GST paid must be recorded for all expenditures made by your company. This would include among other things GST paid on the purchase of equipment or any operating expenses. Let's have a couple of examples.

Let's say that Moe paid $21,400 for his equipment, including $1,400 of GST instead of the $20,000 previously indicated. The entry would be:

Machinery and equipment	$20,000		
GST	$1,400		
Bank loan		$21,400	

The GST in this entry is debited since it is an amount that is refundable to the company. It is, therefore, an asset of the company.

Now let's look at the purchase of some office supplies on credit for $500 plus GST of $35. The entry would be:

Office supplies	$500		
GST	$35		
Accounts payable		$535	

If we look at the GST general ledger account, we would see:

GST

	Debit	Credit	Balance	
			Debit	Credit
Sale		$17.50		
Machinery	$1,400			
Supplies		$35		$1417.50

The general ledger balance for GST shows a net debit. After all of the transactions were recorded, the government owed Moe money.

Preparing the GST return The GST return reformats the information in your GST account. The total of the GST credited to your general ledger account is reflected as **GST collected**. That is the GST charged to your customers upon sale of merchandise or rendering of services. The total GST debited to your general ledger account is reflected as **input tax credits**. Input tax credits are the total payments of GST made for expenses or the acquisition of assets.

Here is the GST return reflecting the transactions above:

Total GST collected	$17.50
Total input tax credits	<u>$1435.00</u>
Net payable (refund)	<u>($1417.50)</u>

When the total input tax credits exceed the GST collected, a refund results. Refunds are not uncommon, particularly when small businesses are starting up, since expenditures normally exceed revenues for the startup period.

The quick method The government has provided an alternate method to those who wish to avoid the tedium of GST calculations. By this method GST is calculated at a flat rate of sales. The rate varies depending on the nature of your business. For instance, the rate for retailers is 1.5 percent on the first $30,000 of sales and 2.5

percent on the remainder. Other types of businesses would pay a rate of 4 percent on the first $30,000 of sales and 5 percent on the remainder. The quick method is available for companies with up to $200,000 in sales.

Let's take the example of Moe's GST under the quick method. Given his sales of $50,000 – his GST would be:

On the first $30,000 – 4%	$1,200
On the remaining $20,000 – 5%	$1,000
Amount due	$3,200

Frequency of filing The size of your small business determines how frequently GST returns must be filed. These are the rules governing the frequency of GST filings:

* If your company does up to $500,000 per year in sales it need only file annually.
* Quarterly filing is required for companies with between $500,000 and $5,000,000 in sales.
* Any company doing more than $5,000,000 in sales, must file monthly.

Any small business has the option of filing monthly or quarterly. If you fear that you will get too far behind if you are only required to file annually, you may wish to take the government up on that option. On the other hand, even if you are only required to file on an annual basis, you are still responsible to remit instalments each quarter. The annual filing option is one that is intended to provide convenience, not financing. GST collected is considered a **deemed trust**. It is money kept on behalf of the government. Tardiness in filing remittances is not treated kindly.

CHAPTER SIX

Analyzing your income statement and balance sheet

INCOME STATEMENT

There is more to reading your income statement than knowing whether or not your company is profitable.

Not only do you want to know whether you are making money, but you want to know *why* you are making money and *how* you can make more money. Conversely, if you are losing money, you want to know *why* you are losing money and what you can do to turn your business around.

First we'll look at the different types of expenses incurred and the effect they have on a company's income. Then we'll consider some of the operating ratios that are critical to evaluating a company's profitability both by you the owner and outside users of financial statements.

Variable expenses   Variable expenses are those expenses that increase or decrease directly with the level of sales. These items are usually included under the cost of sales category of the income statement. If we look at Moe's Hot Dogs' cost of sales, we see two items which are variable expenses:

Income	
Sales	<u>$50,000</u>
Cost of sales	
Purchases	$15,000
Salaries and wages	<u>$12,000</u>
	<u>$27,000</u>

In this particular case, the expenses that would vary with sales are purchases and salaries and wages. The theory is that every time a sale is made, a unit of material and a unit of labor must be consumed. If the sales aren't there, the material won't be used and staff can be laid off so wages can be reduced. (Of course, there is not a direct correlation between wages and sales since it is not so easy to fire and rehire staff every time the factory has a lull. Companies certainly do have layoffs during slow periods, however, and take into account the labor cost per unit of sales when setting their sales prices.)

It is essential for your small business to determine unit cost of production if you are to have any idea on how to price product. In Moe's case, his unit cost of production is 27,000/50,000 or $0.54. In other words, for every dollar of sales revenue, $0.54 of direct manufacturing costs are incurred.

Gross profit percentage This is the ratio that indicates the amount each dollar of sales contributes to your company's profit. It is determined by a simple formula:

Gross profit percentage = 1 – cost of sales percentage
In Moe's case, the gross profit is 1 – 0.54 or 46 percent. In simplest terms, for every extra dollar of sales, Moe increases his net income by 46 cents.

Fixed expenses Fixed expenses are those expenses that don't vary with the level of sales. For instance, rent on the premises stays constant regardless of the level of sales. In addition, office salaries would not be expected to vary directly with the level of sales. Of course, if your company triples in size, no expense would be exempt from some variation, but for most small businesses, fixed costs are a constant.

The notion of fixed costs is very helpful in running a business since it provides you with a level beneath which sales cannot fall if the company is to remain profitable. This level is referred to as the **break-even point**. It is calculated by dividing the fixed costs of running the enterprise by the gross profit percentage. The break-even point is the point at which the business neither earns a profit nor incurs a loss.

Let's calculate the break-even point for Moe's. Before we do this, let's first reproduce a list of his fixed costs:

Overhead

Rent	$5,000
Utilities	$7,000
Legal and accounting	$3,000
Repairs and maintenance	$2,000
Depreciation	<u>$2,000</u>
	<u>$19,000</u>

This list tells Moe that, regardless of the level of sales he makes, $19,000 of expenses will be incurred in the year.

His break-even point would be ($19,000/.46)=$41,304. This means that if Moe achieved $41,304 in sales, his company would break even. The result is easily proven. At $41,304 in sales, his gross profit is ($41,304 x .46)=$19,000, which is the exact amount of his overhead. As we can see, at this level Moe neither earns a profit nor incurs a loss.

Warning signs

The following warning signs should be acted on quickly by anyone running a small business:

1. **An unexpected decline in sales** Declines in sales are often responsible for a decline in the company's financial health. Companies normally need a certain level of sales to stay healthy. If there is evidence of a serious decline in sales, you must quickly determine the reason and plan a course of action.

2. **A decline in the gross profit percentage** This can happen if customers demand increasingly large discounts or if the cost of purchases or wage increases are not adequately priced into the product. It can also occur from inefficiencies in the manufacturing process or problems in a consultant's time-billing system.

3. **A dramatic increase in overhead** This normally occurs from simple overspending. Owners sometimes forget that the many little purchases made each day can add up to big expenses at year-end. Controls on non-essential spending may be needed.

4. **Overhead increases for reasons beyond management's control** Examples are a large rent increase or an increase in interest rates. Savings in other areas, or an increase in sales can compensate for increases like these.

BALANCE SHEET ANALYSIS

As we mentioned previously, the balance sheet of a company represents its financial position at a fixed point in time. It reflects what a company owns (its assets), what a company owes (its liabilities) and how it is financed (how much long-term debt, how much short-term debt and how much equity). What follows is a list of financial benchmarks and ratios relevant to you and to outside users of the company's financial statements.

Working capital Working capital is the amount determined by deducting current assets from current liabilities. It is an important measure of a company's ability to pay its expenses as they become due over the short term. A company must always maintain adequate working capital to maintain credibility with its suppliers and other creditors. A significant investment in heavy equipment or in a building, though contributing to a company's overall wealth, provides little comfort to a supplier or employee waiting for payment. Moe's working capital is as follows:

Current assets	$33,850
Current liabilities	$7,850
Working capital	$26,000

Given the size of Moe's Hot Dogs, the level of working capital is more than adequate to cover expenses in the foreseeable future. Any company with $1.5 in current assets to $1 in current liabilities would be considered financially sound, at least over the short term.

Debt-to-equity ratio Whereas the working capital provides a measure of the company's current position, the debt-to-equity ratio looks at the overall financial position of the company. Many banks and creditors want to know what portion of the operation is financed by debt and what portion financed by equity. This ratio helps to evaluate the overall risk of the enterprise. Clearly if a company is financed primarily by debt, it is far riskier than if it were financed either through earnings or the owner's own funds, the principal reason being that owners will rarely force their own business into bankruptcy, whereas lenders would be far less hesitant to take such action.

The debt-to-equity ratio is calculated by merely dividing the total debt on your balance sheet by the total equity. A healthy company would have a debt-to-equity of one to one. Generally, alarm bells ring if the debt-to-equity ratio of a company exceeds two to one. This means that the company is putting itself in a position where the required debt payments could put too much pressure on the company's operations and working capital.

Let's take a look at the debt-to-equity ratio of Moe's Hot Dogs:

Total liabilities	$27,850
Total equity	$24,000
Debt-to-equity ratio	$27,850/$24,000 = 1.16 to 1

Moe's debt-to-equity ratio is within the healthy range of one to one. At three to one, lenders may begin to get conceived.

Accounts-receivable turnover In assessing the quality of accounts receivable, the accounts-receivable turnover ratio provides considerable information. It lets your backers and creditors know whether the accounts receivable are in line with sales, and ultimately whether they will be largely collectible. A deteriorating accounts-receivable turnover could indicate that your company is lax in collections. This could create serious losses down the road, since substantial write-offs of bad debts can materially affect your income.

A look at Moe's Hot Dogs demonstrates how the accounts-receivable turnover is calculated and how its results are interpreted. First let's reproduce some of the numbers from Moe's financial statements:

Total sales	$50,000
Accounts receivable	$9,600

Turnover is $50,00/$9,600 or 5.21. This means that his accounts receivable are collected in total roughly 5.21 times per year. Put another way, at any given time the accounts receivable contain an average of 70 days of sales (365/5.21). Generally accounts should not exceed a target age of greater than 60 days. As we mentioned earlier, banks will only advance money on accounts receivable that are 60 days old or less.

Warning signs

The following are situations that should be rectified rapidly if they show up on your company's balance sheet:

1. **A deteriorating working capital position** This could occur for any of these reasons:

* Your company is losing money.
* Your company is attempting to repay too much of its long-term debt in too little time. Many entrepreneurs have getting out of debt as their primary objective and try to repay long-term loans ahead of schedule. Often this leaves a serious shortage of operating capital.
* Your company is buying long-term assets with working capital. Generally you should finance major purchases with either long-term debt or an equity contribution. It may be tempting to buy a piece of machinery with a cheque from the bank account, but it may leave the company strapped for cash later.

2. **A decrease in accounts receivable turnover** This could happen for the following reasons:

* Inadequate attention is being paid to the collection of accounts receivable.
* The company is more concerned with making sales than getting paid.
* Some customers are more trouble than they are worth.

3. **A deteriorating debt-to-equity ratio** This could relate to these situations:

* Your company is losing money.

- You are spending too much money on heavy equipment and financing it by debt. Companies that take on too much debt can strangle themselves with large monthly payments.

If your small business gets into trouble, there is no shortage of ways to get helpful advice:

- ask your accountant
- talk to your banker
- go to various government agencies dedicated to helping small business like the Federal Business Development Bank
- get advice from business schools at many universities – MBA students willing to provide consulting services for the experience alone

CHAPTER SEVEN

Other accounting records

Accounting records include not only your books of account and financial reports, but also the source documents from which accounting information is compiled. Source documents are the documents that support or prove transactions, such as:

- purchase or sales invoices
- purchase orders
- banking records – cheques and bank statements
- contractual agreements – leases or franchise agreements

Many of these may be necessary for the resolution of disputes with suppliers or customers. For instance, customers who feel that your books don't accurately reflect a balance owing may request support for the outstanding amount including shipping documents and payment histories.

Government auditors regularly ask for supporting documentation when conducting tax audits. An audit is a verification of records by referencing transactions reported in the books to external evidence. From the government's point of view, unscrupulous entrepreneurs could conceivably create false entries to avoid paying taxes or perhaps to qualify for government grants. Auditors will request supporting evidence to corroborate the bookkeeping records, preferably provided by establishments external to the business. Bank statements, supplier invoices and legal agreements are the documentation they prefer.

Obviously your company must set up a system of storing a host of accounting documentation in addition to the bookkeeping records. Furthermore, it is essential that the records be stored in a manner that makes them easily accessible when needed. Critical documents could cost a business thousands of dollars in lost revenues, tax overpayments or supplier overpayments.

SALES/ACCOUNTS RECEIVABLE

The documents needed to support an amount owing from a customer are:

1. an invoice
2. a shipping document – generally a bill of lading signed by the customer or some detailed evidence of the performance of a service or delivery of goods
3. an account receivable sub-ledger account accurately including all invoices and payments of the customer

It is essential that supporting documentation be easily accessible, so it should be filed in a manner in which it can be easily found. Normally, for sales transactions this is in one of two ways – either by invoice number or by customer. Many companies keep two copies of the customer invoice on hand, one filed by customer with an attached shipping document, and one filed numerically. If a customer calls up accusing you of not delivering the goods for which he is billed, the easiest manner of putting the matter to rest is by presenting him with a supporting shipping document or other similar evidence.

When a government audit is conducted, auditors like to account for the numerical sequence of the invoices to ensure that **all** the sales are recorded. They will often request a numerical file of sales invoices. Furthermore, the numerical file provides management with an alternative control mechanism – by providing a convenient vehicle to ensure that all invoices are accounted for and appropriately recorded.

PURCHASES/ACCOUNTS PAYABLE

The documents needed to support supplier balances are:

1. purchase invoices
2. shipping/receiving documents
3. accounts payable sub-ledger accounts

The key supporting documents for your accounts payable system are supplier invoices together with bills of lading or receiving documents. A filing system should be set up with a folder for each supplier. Miscellaneous files can be maintained by letter for those suppliers with whom you deal infrequently.

BANK STATEMENTS

Every business should have its own independent bank account. The bank account is a key element in ensuring the integrity of your accounting records. It is the control of last resort. Since every transaction must ultimately be settled in cash, the bank statement is the place where virtually every transaction is visible. Every cash disbursement and receipt must eventually clear the bank. It is essential, therefore, to check that the banking records are complete, carefully filed and periodically balanced with the books to ensure their accuracy and the accuracy of your accounting records.

It is folly to try to run a business out of a personal bank account. It is far too easy to confuse transactions between those for your business and those that are of a personal nature. It also makes government authorities suspicious.

In setting up your business bank account, you should make sure your cheques are returned to you every month. There are two reasons for this:

- The cheques provide an essential element of control. They provide support for accounting transactions and deterrence for those who would misuse company funds. Employees would be much less likely to forge signatures if they knew that company cheques would be returned and scrutinized by the owner.
- They provide evidence of the legitimacy of a transaction if other supporting documentation is missing. If a supplier invoice has been misplaced, at least the cheque proves that a payment has actually been made.

In addition to your cheques, you must maintain support for your deposits. Details of each deposit made should be traceable to a deposit record and broken down by their source.

Government auditors immediately assume that all deposits into a company's bank accounts are taxable sales. Tax auditors tend to regard banking records above all others in assessing a company's tax position. If support for a deposit is missing, say a loan you made to your business, it may be taxed as a sale. Alternatively, if you misplace a supplier invoice and don't have a cheque to back up a particular expenditure, an auditor may disallow the expense.

THE BANK RECONCILIATION

Reconciling or balancing the bank is a procedure performed monthly by most well-run businesses. It is a way of checking that your books are in agreement with your banking records. In so doing you ensure that:

- All of your cheques and other cash disbursements are appropriately recorded (Cheques either omitted or improperly recorded will create an out-of-balance condition.)
- All of your deposits are appropriately recorded (Deposits omitted or improperly recorded will create an out-of-balance condition.)
- Any errors uncovered in your books are promptly corrected
- Any errors committed by your bank are promptly corrected (Banks commit many errors of their own that could go undetected for months without the help of a bank reconciliation.)
- All banking transactions were authorized (If a cheque is unrecorded, it may be a fraudulent cheque.)

The bank reconciliation is the process of balancing the cash account in your general ledger with the balance in the business account. The general ledger bank account reflects all of the company's cash disbursements and cash receipts. The bank statement should theoretically contain the identical information. There are usually items on the books that are not on the bank statement and items on the bank statement not included in the books. The reason for this is normally one of timing.

When a company issues a cheque, it will reduce its book balance of cash by the amount of the cheque. The cheque has not yet cleared the bank, however. The supplier to whom the cheque is made has to deposit it in his bank and then it has to clear the company's bank. This could take several days. In other words, there could be several days in which the cheque reduced the company's general ledger cash balance, but did not reduce the bank balance. (It is during this period that the cheque is considered outstanding.) A similar situation can happen with deposits, although this is less frequent.

A third class of transactions may render a bank account out of balance with the books. These relate to bank charges or credits that the bank reflected in the account. It is essential to go through the bank statement at month-end and ensure that these debits or credits are recorded on your books.

 Another point worthy of note here has to do with the nature of bank statements. To throw a wrench into your flawless knowledge of accounting, the bank has reversed the left/right of debits and credits. A debit on the bank statement is a charge and a credit is a deposit. The reason for this rather convoluted occurrence is that the bank statements are prepared from the bank's point of view rather than your point of view. When a bank charges your company's account for a service, they are increasing their own assets while decreasing your company's assets. The same item debited to a bank statement would be credited to a cash account in the general ledger.

Let's take a look at Moe's cash balance at December 31, 2000. Moe's bank account shows a balance of $27,850 and his general ledger balance is $24,250. He has three outstanding cheques totalling $5,200 and an outstanding deposit of $1,600. Here is the bank reconciliation:

Moe's Hot Dogs
Bank Reconciliation
December 31, 2000

Balance per bank	$27,850
Add: Outstanding deposits	<u>$1,600</u>
Subtotal	$29,450
Deduct: Outstanding cheques	<u>($5,200)</u>
Balance per books	<u>$24,250</u>

We can see that outstanding cheques have been deducted since they have already reduced the company general ledger balance (but have not yet cleared the company bank). In order for the two independent sets of records to be in balance, all transactions recorded on one set should be recorded on the other.

The outstanding deposit was added to the bank balance owing to the fact that it had already been included in the general ledger cash account, but was not yet deposited or recorded on the bank statement.

Bank charges are not "reconciling" items since they must be posted directly to the company books by journal entry when the bank statement is received. They are, therefore, deducted by the bank and recorded in the general ledger, so there should be no outstanding difference. Your journal entry to record the monthly bank charges is:

Interest and bank charges	xxx		
Cash in bank		xxx	

HOW LONG SHOULD RECORDS BE KEPT?

The rules regarding the storage of accounting records vary according to the authority with whom you speak. Revenue Canada reserves the right to review records up to **three years** after the end of the fiscal year. Some provincial sales tax statutes require records to be kept up to **six years**. If you fear litigation, 10 years may not be excessive.

If you are looking for a definitive answer, there really isn't one. To be on the safe side, books should be kept for more than five and less than 10 years unless you are planning to acquire a storage shed.

At the conclusion of every fiscal year, after the accountants and auditors have prepared the annual financial statements, the detailed accounting records should be put into storage to make room for those of the coming year. Some companies keep two years of records to provide for any contingency in handling customer and supplier discrepancies, but most of the time it is not good policy to bury your operation in paper. All customer and supplier files together with company books and banking records should be filed away by year in an orderly manner that leaves them readily accessible.

CHAPTER EIGHT

Employees

WHEN IS AN EMPLOYEE AN EMPLOYEE?

There are specific rules governing whether or not an individual is an employee or subcontractor. An employee is a person working under close supervision, who is required to show up for work at designated times, and who uses all the tools and facilities of your business. Subcontractors, on the other hand, may or may not use your premises; they use many of their own tools or supplies and work under limited supervision. The government will look at all the facts surrounding the case to determine if an individual is an employee. Even if your company comes to a mutual agreement with individuals regarding their status as a subcontractor, the government may rule otherwise. What's more, the ruling can be quite costly.

COSTS OF EMPLOYMENT

Employees can be expensive. In addition to basic salaries, there are a host of payroll levies that must be remitted monthly:

Canada Pension Plan (CPP) CPP is levied approximately 3.5 percent on the first $37,000 of your employee's income. The amount calculated is withheld from your employee's pay. You must match the amount withheld with your own contribution. In other words, every dollar of pay you give your employee costs you an additional three and one-half cents.

Employment Insurance (EI) EI is levied at approximately 2.7 percent on the first $39,000 of your employees income. Again as an employer you must make your own contribution to the EI fund equal to 1.4 times the amount withheld from your employee. In other words, every dollar you give your employee costs you an additional (1.4 x 2.7%) $.038 – just shy of four cents.

Workers' Compensation (WC)

Workers' compensation is a form of government insurance given to employees to protect them from the financial loss resulting from a workplace accident. It is calculated as a percentage of employees' income, but is funded entirely by the employer. In other words, there is no payroll withholding. The rates charged range from under $1 per $100 of payroll for office workers, to $10 per $100 for construction workers. The rates relate to the risk inherent in the job.

We can see how these various payroll levies can add up. The total costs per each dollar of pay are $.035 (CPP) + $.038 (EI) + $.04 (WC), or $.113. In other words, every dollar of payroll costs your company about $1.12. It is for this reason that many small business owners like to keep the number of employees on their books to a minimum.

Income Taxes

Income taxes differ from the preceding levies for two reasons:

1. They are paid for entirely by the employee – there is no employer portion to remit.
2. The amount withheld increases with the level of salary and varies with the number of dependents. The CPP, EI and WC rates stay consistent regardless of the salary level, but income tax increases as a percentage of salary as the wages increase.

The government provides tables to determine the amount of income tax to be withheld from an employee's paycheque. The tables are to be used in conjunction with a TD1 form. The TD1 form estimates an employee's annual taxable income and mandates the required deduction as indicated on the withholding tables.

YOUR MONTHLY REMITTANCES

For most small businesses, total remittances are calculated by month and remitted on the 15th day of the following month. For example, your September remittances would be due on October 15. If you are even one day late in submitting your payment, a 10 percent penalty is levied. Let's take a look at Moe's monthly remittances.

Moe has one employee, Lev. Lev is paid $200 per week, and has the following withholdings for the month of January:

Week of:	Wages	CPP	EI	FIT
Jan. 8	$200	$7	$5.6	$25
Jan. 15	$200	$7	$5.6	$25
Jan. 22	$200	$7	$5.6	$25
Jan. 29	$200	$7	$5.6	$25
	$800	$28	$22.4	$100

Lev's weekly net pay would be $162.40 ($200 – $7 – $5.6 – $25). Moe has effectively collected Lev's remittances on behalf of the government. These are considered a **deemed trust**, just as GST is considered a deemed trust.

The journal entry to record weekly payroll would be:

Payroll expense	$200.00	
CPP payable		$7.00
EI payable		$5.60
Income tax payable		$25.00
Cash		$162.40

The liability accounts of CPP and EI payable reflect the fact that tax is collected on behalf of the government and must ultimately be remitted to the government. The credit to cash reflects the paycheque, and the amount charged to wages is the gross pay.

Moe's monthly remittance would be:

CPP	$28 + $28	$56
EI	$22.4 + (1.4 x $22.4)	$54
Income tax		$100
Total		$210

The monthly remittance would be recorded as:

	Debit	Credit	
CPP payable	$28.00		
EI payable	$22.40		
Income tax payable	$100.00		
Payroll burden	$60.00		
Cash		$210.40	

The payroll burden is the company portion of the CPP and EI payable. At the completion of this entry the outstanding payable deductions are eliminated and an expense is set up for the company portion of payroll levies.

ADVANTAGES OF SUBCONTRACTING

As we can see from the preceding example, employing people involves complications. Many of these can be eliminated if subcontractors are employed rather than full-time staff. Here are some advantages of subcontracting:

1. The elimination of tedious bookkeeping. The maintenance of payroll records can be time-consuming and tedious. In addition to calculating the monthly remittances, T4 earning slips must be prepared for all employees at the end of the year. If subcontractors are used, no government remittances are necessary.

2. You save the payroll burden. As we mentioned earlier, the payroll burden can range between 8 percent and 15 percent of the total payroll. The use of subcontractors eliminates this expense.

3. There is ease of termination. Dismissing an employee can be

stressful and expensive. Aside from the legally required severance pay (which can be between two weeks and a month), there is the possibility of being sued for wrongful dismissal. Dismissing a subcontractor can sometimes be as easy as telling them to stop work on a project – so long as you are careful in your contract language.

Caution is important As we mentioned previously, the decision to use a subcontractor may not be your own. It will depend on the needs of your business and the nature of your relationship with a particular individual. People cannot arbitrarily enter into a relationship that violates laws and regulations.

The following would legitimize the subcontracting relationship:

1. Subcontractors have their own offices.
2. They have other clients with whom they work on the same basis.
3. They do not work under close supervision.
4. They do not work at your premises.
5. They use their own tools and equipment.
6. A contract specifying terms of employment is prepared, including the fact that subcontractors are not employees or entitled to the benefits of full-time employment.

Although *all* of the above are not essential in determining a subcontracting relationship, the more of them that are present the stronger the case.

HOW AND WHEN DO YOU GET PAID?
The reason for going into business is to earn income. If you can't draw a salary, there was no point in doing all that work in the first place. The manner in which you are paid depends on the way your business was set up. Generally if you did not incorporate your company, any drawings you take out during the year are treated as a reduction of capital and are not taxable. You pay tax on the income of your business at the conclusion of your year, but no tax is remitted as you draw money out during the year.

Incorporation changes the situation. You can be an employee

of your own corporation. If you draw a salary, you would follow the rules governing remittances for all of your employees with two exceptions – EI and WC. As an owner-manager, you are not required to pay these levies on your salary. You do have the option of paying WC, but you cannot ensure your earnings under EI as an owner-manager. More detail is provided on incorporating in chapter 12.

Computers Computers greatly simplify the payroll function, particularly if you have a number of employees. Virtually all computer programs come with a payroll module. Within the module you will input all relevant information about an employee including deduction level, hourly or weekly wage and pay period. The computer will automatically print the payroll cheque and update all relevant general ledger accounts. It will also provide you with information on the outstanding remittance owing at month-end and prepare the annual T4s and government-filing summaries.

Owing to the fact that taxation rates are constantly changing, all major software companies provide annual updates. These are available at a fraction of the program purchase price.

CHAPTER NINE

Profit planning and projections

Profit planning is a fancy word for budgeting. You already have experience with household budgets. The process begins with determining total household income, allocating it between essential expenses and then determining what is left over for leisure and saving. Your business budget works in much the same way, except that the amount of revenue is generally less certain than in the household and what would be spent on luxury items in the house should normally be retained in the business for future growth.

Your small business budget is basically an income statement for a future period. It is broken down into the same components as the income statement and should be compared to the income statement at the end of the period. By comparing the actual results with the budget, it is possible to determine which elements of income were out of line with the budget and what improvements are required.

THE SALES FORECAST

The sales forecast is the most significant component of your budget primarily because it has such a material effect on your company's expenses. Without a reasonable estimate of sales, you have no idea how much inventory or supplies to buy or how many staff to hire. Other overhead expenses such as rent are directly tied to the sales budget. Obviously a premises adequate to house an operation producing 100,000 widgets a year will differ materially from one producing 5,000,000 per year.

Aside from being the most critical piece of information, sales is also the most difficult to estimate. However, entrepreneurs must have an idea of the size of the market they plan to serve and how much of it they can anticipate capturing. Furthermore, for companies in business for a long period of time, the level of sales should be predictable within reasonable parameters. Sales projections for new companies are the riskiest, owing to the lack of historical information.

A solid sales forecast consists of:

- an assessment of current market and economic conditions
- a review of the company's pattern of growth over the last few years (where available)
- conversations with customers about planned purchasing for the coming period

Regardless of the perils of inaccuracy, particularly with new companies, the forecasting process provides an essential exercise to review your overall strategies, the markets you are participating in and the likely response to your products. It also provides interested third parties such as banks and other creditors with evidence of the seriousness, commitment and competence of the business's owners.

EXPENSES

The budget for expenses is far less difficult to prepare than that for sales. For one thing, many expenses are fixed by agreement, such as those for loan interest, rent or equipment leases. Other expenses, though not predetermined by contract, can be estimated with reasonable accuracy, such as office salaries, telephone and utilities, stationery and office supplies.

Still other expenses are tied directly to the level of sales. These vary for two reasons:

1. As the level of sales increases, so do these expenses. An example of this would be wood expenses for a house builder. A house builder uses more wood if he builds more houses.
2. The unit costs of commodities can vary widely over time. In the case of a house builder, the cost per board foot of lumber could increase dramatically over the course of a year.

The expense portion of the budget must be prepared with reference to all available information. The starting point is with sales. From this the company can determine its raw material and staff requirements. It should then run through the overhead expenses item by item and use all available information in budgeting each one.

It is necessary to update budgets when costs vary to the point where the underlying assumptions of the budget become irrelevant, for instance, if the unit costs of manufacture increase dramatically over the course of the year, or the sales are so great that the company has to move into larger premises.

Moe's Hot Dogs
Projected Statement of Income ($)
For the eight months ended August 31

	Jan.	Feb.	Mar.	Apr.	May.	Jun.	Jul.	Aug.	Total
Sales	6,000	6,000	8,000	8,000	9,000	9,000	10,000	10,000	66,000
Cost of sales									
Purchases	1,800	1,800	2,400	2,400	2,700	2,700	3,000	3,000	19,800
Wages	1,440	1,440	1,920	1,920	2,160	2,160	2,400	2,400	15,840
Total	3,240	3,240	4,320	4,320	4,860	4,860	5,400	5,400	35,640
Gross profit	2,760	2,760	3,680	3,680	4,140	4,140	4,600	4,600	30,360
Overhead									
Rent	450	450	450	450	450	450	450	450	3,600
Utilities	600	600	600	600	600	600	600	600	4,800
Legal	250	250	250	250	250	250	250	250	2,000
Repairs and maintenance	200	200	200	200	200	200	200	200	1,600
	1,500	1,500	1,500	1,500	1,500	1,500	1,500	1,500	12,000
Net income	1,260	1,260	2,180	2,180	2,640	2,640	3,100	3,100	18,360

Moe has derived his **sales figures** from a number of places. First and foremost he looked at his prior-year figures to determine what he could reasonably expect for the coming year. His prior period also helped him to spot seasonal patterns. January and February are the slowest months for most businesses. Sales slowly pick up until they peak in the summer. Moe took the extra precaution of going to some of his bigger customers and asking them to provide him with an idea of the level of their purchases.

Moe used percentages to calculate the **cost of sales**. He assumed that his material purchases would remain at 30 percent of his sales price and that his wages would remain at 24 percent in accordance with his recent experience. Wages are tricky owing to the fact that it is difficult to hire and fire staff in direct proportion to sales. Manufacturing wages are generally hourly, however, allowing certain flexibility in laying off staff in slack periods. A careful monitoring of labor utilization will allow your company to keep costs in a fairly close relationship with sales.

Moe derived his **overhead** figures from the results of operations of his most recent period. They provide him with guideposts of how much he can expect to incur in each of the different expense categories. You will notice that the expenses remain consistent from month to month independent of the level of sales. These are the fixed costs we discussed previously. Regardless of the level of sales obtained, these costs have to be incurred just to keep the doors open.

Let's run down the various overhead expenses and explain how Moe calculated them:

Rent Rent was calculated based on the actual lease agreement with the landlord.

Utilities These were based on last year's experience on a month-to-month basis. They will most likely increase to some degree with the level of sales, but the increase won't materially affect the budget.

Legal and accounting These are budgeted based on prior years' experience. Generally, unless there is a large variation in the professional needs of a business between years, they will stay the same.

Repairs and maintenance Again this expense may vary to some extent based on volume. The variation in this case is not anticipated to be material.

You may be wondering why the budget is prepared on a monthly rather than annual basis. Remember that the budget is a management tool to be used in administering the business. It is important to control costs and revenue on an interim basis. If the results are only monitored annually, it is possible for operations to run out of control for a long time prior to management's being informed and having an opportunity to take any corrective action.

PROJECTED STATEMENT OF CASH FLOW

All but the smallest businesses require a line of credit. In fact, it's rare to find a company that doesn't need to have one. There will be times when it is difficult to collect accounts receivable, or when the company has to increase its inventory for a busy season. In order to stay in business, the company will have to augment its cash flow with the help of the bank. In order to do this, banks often require what is called a projected statement of cash flow. The cash flow statement allows the bank to see when the peak financing requirements of the company occur and whether the company has the capacity to repay them. Banks require a cash flow statement from most new companies or existing companies that want to substantially increase their credit line. (The bank's annual review of an existing credit arrangement rarely requires a cash flow.)

As we noted earlier, expenses are often incurred and revenues earned in advance of their being settled in cash, so even profitable companies can occasionally run into cash flow problems. To prevent this from happening, companies often prepare a cash budget – sometimes called a statement of cash flow. It is a statement formatted in a similar manner to the income statement, with the exception that the expenses and revenue included are paid or settled in cash in the month shown.

It's time to refer back to our old friend Moe. In preparing the statement of cash flow we are going to make the following assumptions:

1. Sales are collected within 30 days. Although this is not borne out by Moe's experience of the prior year, this year we are assuming that he is tightening up on his collection policies.
2. Expenses are incurred on credit (other than wages, which are paid as incurred, and rent, which is paid at the beginning of the month.) Again as with sales, we are going to assume that all outstanding accounts payable are settled within 30 days.
3. For simplicity's sake we are going to start our cash flow projection in February, thereby illustrating the relationship of the projected statement of income to the statement of cash flow.

Moe's Hot Dogs
Projected Statement of Cash Flow ($)
For the seven months ended August 31

Cash provided by:	Feb.	Mar.	Apr.	May.	June.	July.	Aug.	Total
Sales	6,000	6,000	8,000	8,000	9,000	9,000	10,000	56,000
Cash used for:								
Wages	1,440	1,920	1,920	2,160	2,160	2,400	2,400	14,400
Purchases	1,800	1,800	2,400	2,400	2,700	2,700	3,000	16,800
Rent	450	450	450	450	450	450	450	3,150
Utilities	600	600	600	600	600	600	600	4,200
Professional	250	250	250	250	250	250	250	1,750
Repairs and maintenance	200	200	200	200	200	200	200	1,400
	4,740	5,220	5,820	6,060	6,360	6,600	6,900	41,700
Increase in cash	1,260	780	2,180	1,940	2,640	2,400	3,100	14,300
Cash balance beginning	10,000	11,260	12,040	14,220	16,160	18,800	21,200	10,000
Cash balance ending	11,260	12,040	14,220	16,160	18,800	21,200	24,300	24,300

Moe started his cash flow statement in February since that is the month in which many January transactions were settled in cash. Remember that we proceeded on the assumption that sales made on credit and purchases made on credit were settled in 30 days. All expenses incurred except for wages and rent were paid in the month following their billing, for instance, purchases made in January were paid in February. Professional fees incurred in January were likewise paid in February. Similarly, sales made in January were settled in February.

In converting our income statement to a cash flow statement, we then had to display income and expenses when they were settled in cash. At the end of each month we kept a running tab of our bank balance. We started with an opening balance of $10,000. This figure was chosen solely for the purpose of simplicity. It cannot be tied into the preceding balance sheet.

The difference between revenue received and expenses paid is the net change in cash for the month. It must be added to the cumulative cash figure. In the final column you will note that we went back to the initial $10,000 as the beginning cash balance. This is because the final column represents transactions for the entire year to date. The balance at the beginning of the year was the same as the balance at the beginning of the first month.

BUSINESS PLAN

The business plan is a more comprehensive version of the financial projections. It not only includes numbers and assumptions about how the business will proceed, but it contains more comprehensive information on the company, its management, history, product and the market it serves. It also includes information on strategy and competitive advantage about other products and services in the marketplace.

Business plans are generally not necessary when obtaining financing from a bank, large suppliers and landlords. For them, the financial statements and projections will normally be more than enough. Business plans are generally used when companies want creditors to take more than a normal level of risk or when they want outside investors to share in the entrepreneurial risks and returns of an enterprise. In the latter situation the individuals providing capital are more appropriately referred to as investors.

Investors tend to have more interest in the viability of the product and the strength of the management team than any historical financial results. Historical results, however, do provide information on the company's previous success and some indication of its potential to achieve future success.

Always prepare a cash flow budget

Too often small businesses seem to be running blind. Shortages of cash and the stress that accompanies this problem are common – and often unforseen. A **cash flow budget** will enable you to anticipate shortages and take corrective action, either by arranging for additional financing ahead of time or by setting aside cash for future demands. A little advance planning can save both you and your creditors much stress.

CHAPTER TEN

Your system of accounting controls

Internal controls are the system of checks and balances that should be built into your accounting system to ensure that money or other assets are not lost solely due to sloppy administrative procedures and safeguards. It's tough enough to succeed in business when your internal organization is perfect, but if you compound the difficulty with an ineffective accounting system, your odds decrease significantly. There are several ways in which assets can *leak* out of your business. Here are a few:

1. Orders are misplaced and customers not served owing to a chaotic order-entry system.
2. Goods are shipped but not invoiced.
3. Suppliers are paid several times for the same invoice.
4. The bookkeeper opened up her own bank account and deposited company cheques in it and then falsified company records to cover it up.
5. The bank erroneously charged your account for someone else's loan payments.
6. Employees were writing themselves cheques out of the company bank account.
7. Inventory was stolen out of the back during off-hours.

These are just a few of the problems that can undermine the profitability of a small company. Accounting is not solely a science of measurement, it is also an essential tool in the safeguarding of company assets. Let's consider the control function in more detail and look at some simple procedures that can greatly enhance an accounting control system:

Matching shipping documents to sales invoices This is a technique used to ensure that all client orders that are shipped are invoiced. Reviewing unmatched orders in the factory can often indicate orders that have not been billed. If your business happens to be a consulting business, a parallel control could be put in place by keeping detailed time records for yourself and ensuring that they are appropriately billed.

Reviewing bank statements This seems obvious, but is very often not done. This technique involves reviewing the items charged to the bank and flipping through the cleared cheques when they are received from the bank. It is a quick way of ensuring that there are no errors either committed by the bank or staff, and that all the cheques issued are bona fide and reasonable.

Review accounts receivable ledgers One easy way of enforcing control over the sales, accounts receivable, and cash receipt function is by vigilantly monitoring the company's outstanding accounts receivable. Follow up on balances that don't make sense. For instance, if you know that a particular supplier pays promptly but suddenly has a large number of overdue invoices, this may result from receipts charged to the wrong account, or an unscrupulous employee taking company cheques and depositing them in an account under his own control. If an account is in credit balance it may mean that an invoice wasn't recorded.

Review accounts payable subsidiary ledger By reviewing the accounts payable ledger you can gain a degree of comfort that supplier accounts are in line with expectations and that large payments have been accounted for. For instance, if a large payment was made to a particular supplier and the balance remains outstanding, it would indicate that there is a problem with the system (with a concurrent risk that some amounts would be paid twice). Debit balances in the accounts receivable listing should be followed up quickly since this could be an indication that a supplier was paid twice.

Segregation of duties This is the procedure of insuring that individual employees are not in the position to commit and conceal a crime. It splits up duties in such a way that employees keep each other in check. For instance, one employee would prepare the bank reconciliation and the other record the accounts receivable. The same employee should not be responsible for recording the accounts receivable and making bank deposits. This type of control only exists where a company has several employees in the office. In the absence of this, the owner-manager must vigilantly review accounting records and participate in the accounting procedures in such a way as to maintain control.

Preparation and scrutiny of management reports This procedure extends not only to the accounts receivable and accounts payable records referred to above, but also to the financial statements. If it is not possible for you to exercise control with the implementation of separation of duties, it is important to maintain global control through scrutiny of accounting information. The income statement, in particular, provides information about expenses or percentages that are out of line, which could relate to accounting errors or irregularities.

Note that this procedure is facilitated by the use of computers. Every transaction that is input in the computer automatically updates all of the accounting records and compiles the company's financial statements. It is then possible to run off income statements and balance sheets daily if desired. This provides a tremendous vehicle of accounting control.

CHAPTER ELEVEN

Special tips for a consulting business

Consulting businesses are the fastest growing segment of the Canadian economy. Most consulting businesses are quite small – from one to three employees. Many of the owners of these companies are former executives or technicians employed in large companies that were downsized. As we noted in the chapter on employees, the costs and perils of hiring full-time staff can be considerable. Many large companies find it far easier to hire consultants to do much of the work previously done by full-time staff.

As we noted in chapter 8, a consultant must take care to ensure that the relationship between herself and her client is not in fact an employee-employer relationship. If the latter is the case, the benefits of self-employment will be eliminated, and substantial tax penalties may result.

You can prove the legitimacy of your "independent contractor" status by:

1. employing several full-time staff to assist you
2. maintaining an independent office
3. working independently with little supervision
4. incuring the costs of performing the work (you use your own computer, purchase your own office equipment, etc.)

KEEP YOUR BUSINESS SEPARATE

Because your consulting business is small, it is tempting to treat it as an extension of your personal affairs. For example, you may use a computer that you use for other purposes, put your office in the bedroom, or decide it isn't important to maintain a separate bank account. Generally, personal living expenses are considered non-deductible. If you try to write off the couch in your living room because you use it as a reception area, chances are it will be disallowed.

It is important to clearly segregate business from personal expenses:

1. Have an official office that can't be used for any other purpose. If this is a room in your house, it should be used **only** for business and not for personal purposes.
2. Maintain a separate bank account. It may be convenient to use a personal account, but the risk increases that business and personal expenditures will become hopelessly intertwined.
3. Use one specific credit card for miscellaneous expenses. Try not to use cash to pay expenses since it could result in the loss of available deductions. Credit cards and cheques provide additional support for expenses and protect against the inadvertent loss of receipts. If it can be avoided, don't incur personal expenses on a business credit card.

 Keeping track of and legitimizing your business expenses requires properly segregating your business and personal affairs. It also requires the maintenance of proper support for all business transactions. The government will not allow you to claim an expense that isn't adequately supported, or that is of a personal nature.

OTHER TAX CONSIDERATIONS

1. Keep track of your vehicle expenses. It is sometimes best to put all of your vehicle expenses on a single credit card. If that is not possible in all cases – for example, parking – keep an envelope in your car for cash receipts. Lost receipts are lost tax deductions.

2. Keep a mileage log. The government has taken to disallowing auto mileage that can't be substantiated. It is important to maintain support for that portion of mileage that relates to your business.

3. If your office is in your home, keep all utility, tax and mortgage receipts. Remember that you are allowed to deduct a home office expense. At the end of the year you will add up the total costs of carrying your house and deduct that percentage of the total relating to your office.

4. Keep all entertainment receipts. There is generally space on the back of your credit card chits for information on which clients joined you for the meal. You should fill these out since government auditors like to ensure that business meals are bona fide.

5. Keep a separate business telephone line – If your office is in your house, you want to make your business as legitimate as possible. Furthermore, using your home phone for business purposes may make it more difficult to write off business calls.

BILLING CLIENTS

The previous example of Moe's Hot Dogs related to a manufacturing business. Although many of the accounting issues addressed are the same for all small businesses, consulting businesses differ in one major area – revenue.

Manufacturing businesses sell a product. Control is exercised by ensuring that a bill is prepared each time product is shipped. For consultants, the concern is in ensuring that all time is appropriately charged. The product that consultants sell is time. There are only so many hours in a day. It is critical in running a successful consulting business to maximize the return on your time.

You want to ensure that all your time is billed. This is accomplished by what is called a **time-billing system**. With it, your time is accounted for periodically and clients are billed. The time-billing system can be an informal system whereby you merely transcribe your daily time records from a diary to a ledger filed by client, and then prepare a bill from that ledger. The ledger can be as informal or as formal as you like, as long as you have a disciplined way of keeping track of and billing your time.

Example of Time Sheet – Curly's Consulting

Client	Time	Rate	Amount	Description
Jack's Poultry	1.5	100/hr	$150	General consulting
Gerry's Hot Feet	2.5	100	$250	Profit planning
Moe's Hot Dogs	3.0	100	$300	Tax planning
Leon's Bunions	2.0	100	$200	Profit planning
	9.0		$900	

One alternative to the informal system is a computerized system. Time-billing software is available in which time is posted to a "work in process" ledger in the computer and then billed to your client at month-end. The software prepares the invoice and actually prepares an accounts receivable list by client and a journal entry for posting to the general ledger.

Time-billing software generally costs about $200, so it is hardly expensive. On the other hand, for those of you who have a limited roster of accounts, the less formal system probably makes a lot more sense.

CHAPTER TWELVE

To incorporate or not to incorporate

One of the major decisions that you will face at some point in the life of your business is whether or not to incorporate. Incorporation is the act of giving a business its own *legal identity*. When a business is incorporated the assets of the business vest in the corporation, not the individual who was the previous owner. In addition, debts of the business are now debts of the corporation rather than the owner's. The owner of the business can no longer treat the assets as his own and creditors of the business can no longer attack the assets of the individual owner in the event that a debt goes unpaid.

When a business is not incorporated, it is (with few exceptions) not legally distinct from its owner. In other words, assets of the business legally vest in the business-owner. Similarly, creditors of the business can settle their debts out of the personal assets of the business-owner.

One obvious advantage of incorporation is the notion of limited liability. Often you have heard of corporations referred to as limited companies. This is derived from the old concept that corporations limit the claim of creditors to the assets of the business. This is not entirely true today, but it remains a general benefit of in corporation.

Another major advantage of incorporating is in taxes. For instance, income earned in a corporation may be taxed at a much lower rate than income earned personally. Remember that the net income of unincorporated businesses is included in determining your personal taxable income. As a sole proprietor you could pay more than 50 percent tax on the profits of your business. Tax on the first $200,000 of corporate profit, however, is limited to a mere 25 percent, depending on the province (with variations between provinces). The savings are obviously considerable. In addition, special tax breaks may be available upon succession when businesses are incorporated.

Incorporating is a complicated process. It requires hiring a legal professional to set up the corporate entity and then taking a series of steps to ensure that the continuation of the business as a corporation is bona fide. It also requires additional annual governmental filings. Since corporations have a separate legal personality they are required to file their own tax and information returns. What's more, these tend to be more onerous than those required when businesses are unincorporated. They normally require the services of a qualified accounting professional and the retention of a lawyer. Annual professional fees will normally exceed $1,500.

In addition, transactions between you and your corporation are now transactions between two separate legal entities, which must be carefully planned in order to avoid potential tax exposure. For instance, if the owner of a company wants to withdraw extra money for Christmas, the drawing itself may trigger a tax liability.

Tax planning is much more complex with corporations. Along with the opportunities for dramatic tax saving comes added difficulty. Sometimes tax planning involves a series of what appear to be arbitrary transactions. The complexity involved really prohibits nonprofessionals from making these decisions on their own.

 The tax savings from incorporation can be considerable. Every situation is different, however, and care must be taken prior to making the decision. A bad decision could be very costly. Review your business affairs with your accountant to determine if and when incorporation should be undertaken.

Let's summarize some advantages and disadvantages of incorporating.

Advantages	Disadvantages
• limited liability – creditors are restricted to settling claims out of the assets of the business	• more complexity – the creation of a separate legal entity creates more complications in bookkeeping
• substantial tax savings – for a profitable business, the tax savings can be substantial	• more expensive to maintain – different professionals must be retained to incorporate, ensure that the books are properly set up, prepare the annual corporate financial statements
• tax savings and simplicity on succession – ease of succession can be afforded beneficiaries if a company is incorporated	
	• greater exposure to tax problems – with the added tax savings comes added complexity

SHOULD CONSULTANTS INCORPORATE?

The sole reason for the incorporation of consultants is tax savings. Since many consulting businesses are very small and run out of the owner's premises, the restriction on creditors' claims is not a significant issue. Tax savings can be very significant, however, particularly if your business is highly profitable.

The government is concerned about those situations where an individual, who would otherwise be considered an employee, incorporates to save tax. This is similar to the conditions imposed on self-employment discussed in chapter 8. It is a question of fact whether or not an individual is operating as a consultant or as an employee. Particular care must be taken if incorporation is envisioned. The **personal service business** (an incorporated employee) is taxed at the highest rate of corporate tax (50 percent) and denied many deductions. It is a penalty provision used to ensure that you pay your fair share of tax.

In addition to the other tests, the government applies the 67 percent test to determine if a company is a personal service business. If more than two-thirds of your gross revenue is derived from one source, the government will look more closely at the situation. Although this criterion by itself would not necessarily imply that you're not an independent contractor, it does not help your case. Additional care must be taken when considering incorporating your consulting business.

ACCOUNTING FOR DIFFERENT TYPES OF BUSINESS ENTITIES

To understand the differences in accounting for an incorporated entity, as opposed to an unincorporated entity, we must first understand the effect that incorporation has on the accounts. One of the major changes relates to the classification of the owner's investment in his company. When an owner invests money in his corporation, he can do it either through issuing himself capital stock of the company, or *lending* the money to the company.

This is a considerable advantage over unincorporated entities. In the latter case, owners could not treat themselves as creditors of the company and could only pay themselves after all other creditors were paid in the event the company was discontinued. In the case of incorporated entities, however, owners can *lend* money to the company and be treated with all the rights of other creditors of the business.

The process of issuing capital stock is similar to the capital contribution made by a sole proprietor to his unincorporated business. Just as the sole proprietor must repay all his creditors before taking back his interest in the business, the shareholder is the last to get paid if the company is dissolved. Similarly a capital contribution made by an owner to an unincorporated business is not considered a debt of the business, but rather equity in the business.

Let's say Moe decided to incorporate. Let's further assume that he did it at the outset, rather than one year after he commenced operations. In our example, Moe invests $20,000 in his company, $5,000 as equity and the balance as a loan to the company. Here is the journal entry recording the transaction:

Cash	$20,000		
Capital stock		$5,000	
Shareholder's loan		$15,000	

Moe now has equity in his company of $5,000 and a liability owing to him of $15,000. Assuming no other transactions, his balance sheet would be:

Assets		**Liabilities**	
Cash	$20,000	Shareholder's loan	$15,000
		Equity	
		Capital stock	$5,000
			$20,000

A contribution to an unincorporated entity is recorded as:

Cash	$20,000		
Proprietor's capital		$20,000	

A proprietor cannot be a creditor to his unincorporated entity since it is not possible to lend money to yourself and then legally enforce collection.

One other difference between corporations and unincorporated entities relates to the treatment of the owner's drawings. Since the corporation is a separate legal entity from its owner, drawings are no longer simply a charge against owner's capital. The owner has two choices in how money is withdrawn from both an accounting and tax point of view. One is as payment for services rendered in the same manner as salaries are paid to employees. In this particular case, the drawing would be treated as a salary.

The alternative is to treat the drawing as a return on invested capital, which relates to the ownership of company shares. Taking money out of a company by virtue of ownership is referred to as a dividend and is generally calculated on a per share basis. Dividends are alternatively referred to as a distribution of profits. Salaries are a regular expense in calculating a company's net income and, therefore, appear on the income statement with other expenses. In other words, shareholders of an incorporated entity can pay themselves salaries. The salary is treated as any other expense of the company and is deducted in determining the corporation's income.

The salary/dividend choice is a highly complicated one with many implications from both taxation and legal perspectives. The manner in which money is drawn out of a company can have a profound impact on the amount of tax paid. It is for this reason that Moe needs serious advice from a tax professional before he takes out any cash.

Another item of the equity section of the balance sheet that we didn't discuss is the retained earnings account. This is the accumulated income retained in the business that was not distributed to the owner by way of dividend.

Let's say that Moe has drawn $20,000 out of his corporation; he has decided to treat $10,000 as salary and $10,000 as dividend. Let's further assume that his company had $25,000 in sales and, for simplicity's sake, no expenses.

The journal entry would be:

Salary	$10,000	
Dividend	$10,000	
Cash		$20,000

The entry shows the use of cash in payment of the owner's drawing, half of which was treated as a dividend and the balance salary.

The income statement would appear as:

Sales	$25,000
Expenses	
Salaries	<u>$10,000</u>
Net income	<u>$15,000</u>

The $10,000 dividend would be posted directly to the retained earnings account since it is not an expense but a distribution of profit. The retained earnings account in the general ledger and on the balance sheet would show a balance of $5,000:

Retained Earnings

	Debit	Credit	Balance	
			Debit	Credit
To close the income & expense accounts for the year		$15,000		
To record payment of dividend	$10,000		$5,000	

If Moe were to have drawn out the $20,000 from an unincorporated company, the entry would have simply been:

Owner's capital (equity)	$20,000		
Cash		$20,000	

The owner's drawing would have been charged straight to his capital account since proprietors of unincorporated companies cannot pay themselves a salary and deduct it. This makes sense since there is no legal distinction between the two.

CHAPTER THIRTEEN

Hiring an accountant

One of the most important decisions you make in running a small business is hiring an accountant. Accountants perform many functions critical to managing a small enterprise. They:

1. **provide assistance in setting up your accounting system.** Accountants can provide input and advice on setting up an appropriate manual system, or aid in the selection and set-up of the most appropriate computer software.
2. **can prepare the annual financial statements.** Financial statements require considerable expertise to prepare. Normally entrepreneurs will not have this expertise and will require the services of an outside professional.
3. **help to interpret financial results at the conclusion of the accounting cycle.** Often, statements can be difficult and cumbersome to work with. An accountant can help untangle the web of complexity by explaining the significance of the information you've developed, how your company is doing, whether costs and revenues are in line and what can be done to strengthen your company's financial health.
4. **act as a liaison with the company's bank.** Often difficulty is encountered when interpreting your financial results to the bank. Accountants can help in articulating the company's financial position as well as its goals, aspirations, and financial requirements to your bank.
5. **provide tax-planning advice.** In Canada, where tax rates are high, knowing how to structure your financial affairs to minimize the tax burden is critical. Often, your accountant's

95

principle responsibility will be tax minimization. Entrepreneurs often want to save tax more than anything else and they rely on their accountants for this service beyond all others. They often do so at their own peril, for tax management is a small component of the overall running of the business, and not necessarily the most important one.

6. **assist in the preparation of business plans and budgets for the enterprise.** Your accountant is normally the individual most qualified to prepare these critical documents.

WHAT TO LOOK FOR IN AN ACCOUNTANT

There are number of things to look for in an accountant:

Competence Above all it is important that the accountant you hire knows what he is doing. One of the best ways of ensuring that your accountant has at least a minimum of competence is to check for a professional designation. Generally accountants most qualified to deal with small business are CAs (chartered accountants). Their standards of education and entry requirements are very rigorous and they are the only designation authorized to conduct audits in many provinces. There are other accounting designations such as CGAs (certified general accountants) and CMAs (certified management accountants) who do receive a rigorous education, but may not be licensed to offer the full array of services. The designation alone is not enough to ensure that any particular accountant is the best person available, but it provides an indication of the individual's qualifications.

Knowledge of your business Even if an accountant is competent, a lack of experience in a certain area can result in a less-than-ideal relationship. For example, if like Moe you manufacture hot dogs, you might be well served to have an accountant who has experience in the food-processing business. He will be in the best position to anticipate the specific needs of a given industry, and to spot trends that might be unhealthy or out of line with industry norms.

Type of services Often accountants specialize in certain areas, for example, tax planning. A good accountant for a small business must provide a variety of services, however. A tax accountant may neglect to provide much-needed financial advice, and a management accountant may neglect to perform adequate tax planning. For most small companies, there are plenty of accountants who can wear all the required hats. For those who feel they need specialized assistance in a variety of areas, larger accounting firms with different departments can be retained.

Communication Many accountants differ in their capacity to communicate. Often accountants read through the financial statements at the year-end meetings as though they are reading to themselves. It is essential that you understand what your accountant says so you can act on the information provided.

Like and trust More than any other professional, an accountant is an external friend of the business. It is important that the owner of the business feel comfortable dealing with that person. To get the most out of your relationship, you must be as candid as possible. If you feel you have to hide information from your accountant, you may be depriving yourself of some very valuable input.

Affordability Professional accountants can charge anywhere from $100 to $300 per hour. You should ask the hourly rate of the accountant *and* get an estimate of the amount of time required to service your account. Often senior accountants will delegate to more junior staff to keep the overall fee lower.

Generally the best way of ensuring that an accountant is right for you is through references. If he or she comes recommended from a trusted financial advisor, that alone may provide enough comfort. Banks are a major source of recommendations. Since they are often the principal users of the financial statements outside of government, and certainly have a vested interested in the success of the enterprise, they are in a great position to provide a list of able candidates.

Choosing and dealing with a bank

Just as it is necessary to pick an accountant who is right for your business, so it is necessary to choose your bank, trust company or credit union wisely. Some banks are more aggressive in dealing with small businesses and do not provide the flexibility and support so often needed. Although all banks pay lip service to the importance of their small business services, entrepreneurs find that many banks treat them as an inconvenience and provide services and support only grudgingly. What's more, with much of the restructuring that has occurred in the banking industry of late, the duties heaped on many managers limit their time to deal with small company problems. It is essential, above all, to know that a bank wants and values your business. This will be evident in the way you are treated by the manager, the speed with which they handle your requests and the conditions they put on lending your company money.

It also helps if the bank has experience in dealing with your type of business. Many businesses have different banking requirements; for instance, a retail business may require a bulge in its bank loan just before Christmas to stock up on inventory. A bank manager who doesn't understand your business may be slow to react to its needs.

It is wiser to concentrate on the bank's philosophy of business when choosing the right institution, since any particular individual at a branch will be subject to transfer. You can determine a bank's philosophy by reviewing the services it offers, reading its printed material, having an in-depth conversation with banking people and, if possible, with existing customers. This latter option will only generally be possible if you are referred to the bank by one of its customers.

Here are questions to consider in choosing a bank:

1. **Do you get along with the manager?** Although managers don't stay in particular branches for more than a few years, it is in the first few years of being in business that a good relationship is most critical. Two-thirds of all new business fail in the first three years of operation. To mitigate this risk, good banking relations should be established at the outset.

2. **Is the manager experienced?** Aside from the manager being pleasant, you want a person who is experienced in the ways of the bank. New managers tend to have limited discretion and refer everything to seniors executives in order to get approval. This can be very aggravating, since it can slow down critical decisions.

3. **What kind of security does the bank require?** When banks advance money, particularly to new businesses, they normally require collateral. Collateral is an asset of value pledged to them to ensure they will get paid in full in the event of loan default. Banks are not in the business of taking significant risks. When dealing with a new business, they will require either a collateral mortgage on a house, or some other asset of value.

4. **What services do they offer?** Banks differ with respect to the services they offer to a small business. For instance, at present some banks very more involved in offering Internet banking facilities while others are not.

How do you deal with the bank? Banks are looking to ensure that your business is profitable and that you know what you're doing. They want to be confident that you are aware of what the effects of your decisions have on the company's financial position. They don't like "pie in the sky" plans that aren't grounded in reality. They get nervous when entrepreneurs are too aggressive and focus on growth without understanding the necessity of maintaining a solid financial position.

Many entrepreneurs confuse sales with success. Unfortunately many small businesses overextend themselves and are unable to honor their commitments owing to a chronic shortage of working capital. The normal pattern at this point is to blame the bank rather than take responsibility for inadequate planning.

The best way to keep the bank on your side is to run your business well, controlling costs and anticipating financing requirements, rather than reacting to working capital shortages once they have already occurred. Banks will be generous if they believe in you, the management team.

Here's how to reinforce the bank's faith in the ability of your company:

1. **Have a business plan.** Set specific goals that you want your business to achieve in the short and medium term. Banks, particularly those catering to small business, become somewhat wary if plans extend too far into the future owing to the uncertainty of the small business environment.

2. **Understand your financial statements.** Bank managers and loan officers are trained to understand the meaning of financial statements presented to them. They will ask pointed questions about the information presented. Their comfort will be enhanced if you understand the information you provide or your accountant provides.

3. **Anticipate the bank's concerns and prepare viable answers to them.** If there is a decline in working capital, or if the gross profit percentage has gone down, explain how this has occurred and map out how the company plans to deal with it.

4. **Try to stay within the terms of the banking agreement.** Often banks will specify certain criteria within which they want clients to operate. For instance, they might want a certain level of capital investment to be maintained by the owner. Don't draw out so much money that you leave your company vulnerable.

5. **Prepare an annual budget and go over it with the bank.** This provides the bank with a road map of where your company plans to go over the near term, and what it can do to help its progress.

6. **Stay on top of the accounts receivable.** Ensure that you don't neglect the collection process. Often it is more difficult to collect outstanding accounts that have been outstanding for an extended period of time. Try to keep your accounts receivable within 60 days of age. Follow up regularly with tardy customers. Don't get caught in a trap of providing goods or services to customers with a history of late payments.

7. **Provide all information that the bank requests on a timely basis**. Don't make the bank wait too long for an accounts receivable aging, or the annual financial statements. This affects your credibility. If information is not forthcoming, the bank will get suspicious.

8. **Head off problems before they get too serious.** If you see a financial crunch coming, contact the bank immediately – don't wait until it arrives. Banks will be more receptive to helping entrepreneurs if they feel that they are being dealt with openly and honestly.

9. **Ensure that the financial information provided to the bank is accurate.** Financial information that is nonsensical, or is inconsistent with other realities of the business, will bring into question the credibility of the enterprise and its management. This goes back to the issue of having the right accountant.

10. **Open the lines of communication between your accountant and your bank.** Since the accountant prepares the financial information on which the bank makes its credit decisions, direct access to the accountant can often provide considerable comfort to the bank.

NOTES & UPDATES

NOTES & UPDATES

NOTES & UPDATES